gettyimages

1970s

gettyimages

1970s

Decades of the 20th Century
Dekaden des 20. Jahrhunderts
Décennies du XXe siècle

Nick Yapp

KÖNEMANN

This book was produced by Getty Images
Unique House, 21–31 Woodfield Road, London W9 2BA

For KÖNEMANN*:
Managing editor: Sally Bald
Project editor: Susanne Hergarden
Assistant: Christian Kassung
German translation: Ellen Küppers
French translation: Stéphane Schoonover
Contributing editor: Stéphanie Aurin

For Getty Images:
Art director: Michael Rand
Design: Ian Denning
Managing editor: Annabel Else
Picture editor: Ali Khoja
Picture research: Alex Linghorn
Editor: James Hughes
Proof reader: Elisabeth Ihre
Scanning: Austin Bryan
Production: Robert Gray
Special thanks: Leon Meyer,
Téa Aganovic and Antonia Hille

*KÖNEMANN is a registered trademark of Tandem Verlag GmbH

Printed in Germany

ISBN 3-8331-1083-X

10 9 8 7 6 5 4 3 2 1
X IX VIII VII VI V IV III II I

Frontispiece: The Spirit of the Seventies. A hippie in scant
but full regalia sways to the music at a rock festival at Knebworth,
England, August 1979.

Frontispiz: Der Geist der siebziger Jahre. Ein Hippie, spärlich
bekleidet, doch mit allen Insignien der Hippie-Mode geschmückt,
wiegt sich im Rhythmus der Musik auf dem Rock-Festival in
Knebworth, England, August 1979.

Frontispice : L'esprit des années soixante-dix. Une hippie, presque nue,
mais parée de ses beaux atours, tangue au rythme de la musique du
festival de rock de Knebworth, Angleterre, août 1979.

Contents / Inhalt / Sommaire

Introduction 6
Einführung 8
Introduction 10

1. Movers and shakers
   Spieler und Gegenspieler
   Les progressistes et les
     agitateurs 12

2. Conlict
   Konflikte
   Les conflits 48

3. Terrorism
   Terrorismus
   Le terrorisme 102

4. Issues
   Die großen Themen
   Les grands thèmes 122

5. Cinema
   Kino
   Le cinéma 160

6. The Arts
   Die Kunst
   Les arts 190

7. Pop
   Popmusik
   La musique pop 212

8. Fashion
   Mode
   La mode 242

9. Youth
   Die Jugend
   La jeunesse 264

10. Sport
    Sport
    Le sport 286

11. Children
    Kinder
    Les enfants 322

12. All human life
    Menschliches, Allzumenschliches
    Les petits et grands événements
      de la vie 350

Index 394

Introduction

It was the decade of wonderwomen and supermen. On the distaff side, there was the young Thatcher, Mother Theresa of Calcutta, black activist Angela Davis, and the feminist movement. On the testosterone side, there was Ho Chi Minh, Sylvester Stallone, Muhammad Ali, the Ayatollah Khomeini, and *Jesus Christ Superstar*. Love them or hate them, they were not to be ignored.

Everything and everyone seemed out to polarize opinion. It was not a time for compromise. The IRA bombed themselves into disgrace with carnage in Northern Ireland and mainland Britain. The CIA engineered a coup in Chile. War eventually shut down in Vietnam, but opened in plenty of other theatres: Cambodia, Lebanon, the Middle East, Cyprus and Rhodesia/Zimbabwe. The Shah fled swiftly from Iran. Idi Amin left Uganda less speedily but just as permanently. President Nixon licked his lips and assured Americans that he was honest, but the sweat broke out again as the facts of the Watergate affair became known.

Suddenly, we discovered that we had been inflicting dreadful harm on our planet. There were protests at nuclear plants, fuelled by the Three Mile Island disaster in the USA. People tried to clean up our poisoned seas, but the wreck of the giant oil tanker *Amoco Cadiz* in the Channel didn't help. Inadequate measures were introduced to reduce pollution in the very air we breathed. The inhabitants of Flixborough in Britain had to contend with a cloud of poisonous cyclohexane gas; the inhabitants of Meda in Italy with highly toxic dioxin.

People changed their sex, or at least their avowed sexuality. There were gay rights, women's rights, ethnic rights and animal rights to be considered, and many found that very hard indeed. There were moon buggies and skylabs, pictures from Mars, oil from the North Sea, and babies from test tubes. Hell's Angels dressed in black and shoved metal studs through their leathers. Punks sported every colour of the psychedelic rainbow, but preferred to shove metal studs through their ears and noses. Women wore ra-ra skirts and hot pants. Men wore flares and big collars.

The wrath of God was ever-present, though most of us could have done without it. There were earthquakes in China and Italy, floods in Spain, cyclones in Fiji and Northern Australia. And, where God didn't intervene, our own species was making a mess of things. Arab guerrillas blew up three airliners in Jordan; Basque separatists killed Spanish minister Luis Carrero Blanca; the INLA killed Conservative minister Airey Neave and were alleged to have killed Earl Mountbatten; 11 Israeli athletes were killed by terrorists at the Munich Olympics in 1972. In Jonestown, Guyana, 900 followers of the Reverend Jim Jones committed suicide.

Janis Joplin, Jimi Hendrix and Elvis Presley died. The Beatles broke up. Woody Allen became a star. George Lucas brought us *Star Wars*. Marlon Brando and Francis Ford Coppola brought us *The Godfather*. There were sporting triumphs for Grand National winner Red Rum, athletes Mary Peters and Sebastian Coe, gymnast Olga Korbut, tennis supremo Martina Navratilova, and many others, including a young American footballer named O J Simpson.

Einführung

Die siebziger Jahre waren das Jahrzehnt der Powerfrauen und Supermänner. Auf der Seite der Frauen standen die junge Margaret Thatcher, Mutter Theresa aus Kalkutta, die schwarze Aktivistin Angela Davis und die Feministinnen. Auf der Seite der Männer waren es Ho Chi Minh, Sylvester Stallone, Muhammad Ali, Ayatollah Khomeini und *Jesus Christ Superstar*. Ob man sie nun liebte oder haßte, ignorieren konnte sie niemand.

Zu allem und jedem mußte man sich eine Meinung bilden. Es war kein Jahrzehnt der Kompromisse. Die IRA zerstörte mit ihren Bombenanschlägen in Nordirland und auf dem britischen Festland die Grundlagen für politische Lösungen. Der CIA zog bei einem Militärputsch in Chile die Fäden. Der Krieg in Vietnam war gerade zu Ende, da beherrschten schon neue Kriegsschauplätze die Schlagzeilen: Kambodscha, Libanon, der Mittlere Osten, Zypern und Rhodesien, das heutige Simbabwe. Der Schah floh überstürzt aus dem Iran. Ugandas Herrscher Idi Amin klammerte sich an seine Macht, verließ aber schießlich doch das Land. US-Präsident Nixon versicherte den Amerikanern mit wohlfeilen Worten seine Redlichkeit, doch wurde Lügen gestraft, als die Wahrheit über die Watergate-Affäre ans Licht kam.

Plötzlich mußten wir feststellen, mit welchen Gefahren wir unseren Planeten bedrohten. Der Reaktorunfall von Three Mile Island in den USA hatte die Menschen aufgeschreckt – zahlreiche Proteste gegen Atomkraft waren die Folge. Während man versucht, dem Gift in den Meeren Herr zu werden, läuft der gigantische Öltanker *Amoco Cadiz* im Ärmelkanal wrack. Die Maßnahmen gegen die Luftverschmutzung waren mehr als mangelhaft. So mußten die Einwohner der englischen Stadt Flixborough in einer giftigen Wolke aus Cyclohexangas ausharren; in der italienischen Stadt Meda atmeten die Menschen hochgiftiges Dioxin ein.

Menschen nahmen Geschlechtsumwandlungen vor, oder bekannten sich zumindest zu ihrer wahren Sexualität. Schwule und Lesben forderten öffentlich ihre Rechte, ethnische

Randgruppen pochten auf Anerkennung und man kämpfte für den Schutz von Tieren. Für manche war es gar nicht leicht, sich mit den Erscheinungen der neuen Liberalität anzufreunden. Plötzlich gab es Mondfahrzeuge und Raumstationen, Bilder vom Mars, Öl aus der Nordsee und Babys aus dem Reagenzglas. Das bevorzugte Outfit der Hell's Angels war schwarze, mit Nieten besetzte Lederkleidung. Dagegen präsentierten sich die Punker in allen Regenbogenfarben und steckten sich Metallknöpfe durch Ohren und Nase. Die Damenmode brachte ultrakurze Röcke und Hot Pants hervor, die Herren trugen Pelze und breite Kragen.

Der Zorn Gottes war allgegenwärtig, doch die meisten von uns hätten gut darauf verzichten können: Erdbeben in China und in Italien, Überschwemmungen in Spanien, Wirbelstürme auf den Fidschiinseln und in Nordaustralien. Dort, wo nicht Gott eingriff, richteten die Menschen verheerendes Unheil an: Arabische Terroristen sprengten in Jordanien drei Flugzeuge; baskische Separatisten ermordeten den spanischen Minister Luis Carrero Blanca; der konservative Minister Airey Neave fiel der INLA (Irish National Liberation Army) zum Opfer, die zugleich des Mordes an Graf Mountbatten beschuldigt wurde; während der Olympischen Spiele 1972 in München töteten palästinensische Terroristen 11 israelische Sportler. In Guyana, Jonestown folgten 900 Anhänger ihrem Sektenführer Jim Jones in den Tod.

Janis Joplin, Jimi Hendrix und Elvis Presley starben. Die Beatles gingen auseinander. Woody Allen wurde ein Star. George Lucas faszinierte die Kinobesucher mit dem *Krieg der Sterne*, Marlon Brando und Francis Ford Coppola mit dem *Paten*. Red Rum gewann den Grand National von England. Die Leichtathleten Mary Peters und Sebastian Coe, die Turnerin Olga Korbut und der Tennisstar Martina Navratilova, sie und viele andere, den jungen amerikanischen Football-Spieler O. J. Simpson nicht zu vergessen, feierten ihre sportlichen Triumphe.

Introduction

Ce fut la décennie des femmes d'action et des hommes d'exception. Du côté féminin, il y eut la jeune Thatcher, mère Thérésa, la militante noire Angela Davis et le mouvement féministe. Du côté masculin, il y eut Hô Chi Minh, Sylvester Stallone, Mohammed Ali, l'ayatollah Khomeiny et *Jesus Christ Superstar*. Qu'on les aime ou qu'on les déteste, on ne pouvait les ignorer.

Toutes sortes de choses et de gens semblaient polariser l'opinion. Ce ne fut pas l'époque des compromis. L'IRA se discrédita par ses carnages en Irlande du Nord et en Angleterre. La CIA manigança un coup d'Etat au Chili. La guerre finit par s'achever au Viêt-nam, mais proliféra dans de nombreux autres endroits : au Cambodge, au Liban, au Moyen-Orient, à Chypre et au Zimbabwe (ex-Rhodésie). Le shah d'Iran s'enfuit de son pays. Idi Amin quitta l'Ouganda moins rapidement, mais tout aussi définitivement. Le président Nixon se frotta les mains et assura les Américains de son honnêteté, mais il eut de nouveau des sueurs froides quand l'affaire du Watergate éclata au grand jour.

Nous avons soudain découvert quels maux épouvantables nous infligions à notre planète depuis des années. Des protestations s'élevèrent contre les centrales nucléaires, alimentées par le désastre de Three Mile Island aux Etats-Unis. On essaya de nettoyer les mers empoisonnées, mais le naufrage dans la Manche du pétrolier géant l'*Amoco Cadiz* n'arrangea pas les choses. Des mesures inadéquates furent prises pour réduire la pollution de l'air. Les habitants de Flixborough en Grande-Bretagne durent combattre un nuage empoisonné de gaz cyclohexane ; ceux de Meda en Italie de dioxine hautement toxique.

Les gens eurent la possibilité de changer de sexe; ou du moins de reconnaître leur propre sexualité. On commença à tenir compte des droits des homosexuels, des droits des femmes, des droits des ethnies et des droits des animaux et beaucoup trouvèrent cela vraiment très difficile. Il y eut des véhicules sur la lune et des laboratoires spatiaux « Skylab », des photos de

Mars, du pétrole de la mer du Nord et des bébés-éprouvette. Les Hell's Angels s'habillaient en noir et fourraient des clous dans leurs blousons de cuir. Les punks exhibaient toutes les couleurs de l'arc-en-ciel psychédélique, mais préféraient se fourrer les clous dans les oreilles et le nez. Les femmes portaient des jupes à falbalas et des shorts ultracourts ; les hommes des pantalons à pattes d'éléphant et des cols larges.

Cependant la colère divine planait toujours sur nos têtes et la plupart d'entre nous s'en serait bien passé. Il y eut des tremblements de terre en Chine et en Italie, des inondations en Espagne, des cyclones dans les îles Fidji et dans le nord de l'Australie. Et là où la main de Dieu ne frappa pas, ce sont les humains qui firent des dégâts. Des guérilleros arabes firent sauter trois avions en Jordanie ; les séparatistes basques assassinèrent le ministre espagnol Luis Carrero Blanca ; l'INLA (Irish National Liberation Army) assassina le ministre conservateur Airey Neave et fut accusée d'avoir tué le comte Mountbatten ; 11 athlètes israéliens furent massacrés par des terroristes lors des Jeux olympiques de Munich en 1972. A Jonestown en Guyane, 900 disciples du révérend Jim Jones se suicidèrent.

Janis Joplin, Jimi Hendrix et Elvis Presley moururent. Les Beatles se séparèrent. Woody Allen devint une star. Georges Lucas tourna *La Guerre des Etoiles*, Marlon Brando et Francis Ford Coppola, *Le Parrain*. Il y eut des triomphes sportifs pour Red Rum, le vainqueur du Grand National, pour les athlètes Mary Peters et Sebastian Coe, la gymnaste Olga Korbut, la star de tennis Martina Navratilova, ainsi que beaucoup d'autres, y compris un jeune footballeur américain du nom de O. J. Simpson.

1. Movers and shakers
Spieler und Gegenspieler
Les progressistes et les agitateurs

December 1978. The religious leader who toppled a dynasty – the Ayatollah Khomeini. In Iran, a few weeks later, taped messages smuggled in from the Ayatollah in Paris inspired a wave of strikes that brought an end to the Shah's rule.

Dezember 1978. Ayatollah Khomeini, der religiöse Führer, der eine Dynastie stürzte. Einige Wochen später ließ der Ayatollah von seinem Pariser Exil aus Tonbänder in den Iran schmuggeln, auf denen er zu Streiks und zum Sturz des Regimes aufrief.

Décembre 1978. L'ayatollah Khomeiny, le leader religieux qui renversa une dynastie. En Iran, quelques semaines plus tard, des messages de l'ayatollah enregistrés sur bande et passés clandestinement depuis Paris furent à l'origine d'une série de grèves qui provoqua la chute de l'empire du shah.

1. Movers and shakers
Spieler und Gegenspieler
Les progressistes et les agitateurs

Many world leaders were on the move in the Seventies. President Nixon sought popularity at home by visiting Chairman Mao in China and President Brezhnev in the Soviet Union. Nixon claimed he had 'serious and frank' discussions with both leaders, but frankness was never one of Tricky Dicky's strong points. Henry Kissinger scurried to and fro on Nixon's behalf – to Paris for the Vietnam peace talks in 1974, to Geneva to meet Andrei Gromyko two years later.

Mao himself died in 1976, and Madame Mao and the Gang of Four were arrested. President Bhutto of Pakistan was ousted by General Zia. Ian Smith lost his civil war in Rhodesia/Zimbabwe. President Allende was killed by CIA-backed rebels in Chile. The Lion of Judah, Haile Selassie, was forced to leave Ethiopia in 1974. Franco died and Juan Carlos I became king of Spain. The Shah fled from Iran and General Amin from Uganda in 1979. In 1978 three popes occupied the Vatican throne.

Edward Heath navigated Britain into the European Common Market in 1972, for de Gaulle was no longer there to say 'Non!'. In 1977 Menachem Begin and the right-wing Likud party ended unbroken Labour rule in Israel since the state had been founded 29 years earlier.

Seldom had movers and shakers been so moved and so shaken.

Viele der führenden Staatsmänner waren in den siebziger Jahren auf Reisen. Präsident Nixon besuchte Mao in China und Breschnew in der Sowjetunion, womit er seine Popularität im eigenen Land steigern wollte. Nixon versicherte, er habe mit beiden Staatsoberhäuptern „ernsthafte und offene" Gespräche geführt, doch Offenheit war nie eine der Stärken von Tricky Dicky gewesen. Henry Kissinger stand ihm zur Seite und eilte 1974 in dessen Auftrag zu den Vietnam-Friedensgesprächen nach Paris und zwei Jahre später nach Genf, wo er Andrej Gromyko traf.

Mao starb 1976; seine Frau und die „Viererbande" wurden verhaftet. Präsident Bhutto von Pakistan wurde von General Zia aus dem Land vertrieben. Ian Smith mußte im Bürgerkrieg von Rhodesien, dem heutigen Simbabwe, einsehen, daß die Tage der weißen Vorherrschaft zu Ende waren. Der chilenische Präsident Allende wurde von Rebellen ermordet, die der CIA unterstützte. Haile Selassie, der „Löwe von Juda" mußte 1974 Äthiopien verlassen. Franco starb. Juan Carlos I. wurde König von Spanien. 1979 verließ der Schah den Iran, und General Idi Amin floh aus Uganda. 1978 hatten drei Päpste auf dem vatikanischen Thron gesessen.

Edward Heath führte 1972 England in die Europäische Union, und de Gaulle konnte dazu nicht länger „Nein" sagen. Menachem Begin und sein rechter Flügel der Likud-Partei beendeten 1977 die Herrschaft der Arbeiterpartei, die seit der Staatsgründung Israels 29 Jahre lang das Land regiert hatte.

Selten tauschten Spieler und Gegenspieler so oft ihre Rollen wie in dieser Dekade.

Nombre de leaders mondiaux sillonnèrent la planète dans des années soixante-dix. Le président Nixon voulut augmenter sa cote de popularité en rendant visite à Mao en Chine et Brejnev en URSS. Il prétendit même avoir eu des discussions « sérieuses et franches » avec les deux chefs d'Etat, mais l'honnêteté ne fut jamais le fort de Tricky Dicky. A la demande de Nixon, Henry Kissinger se rendit en toute hâte à Paris, en 1974, pour les négociations de paix du Viêt-nam et deux ans plus tard à Genève pour rencontrer Andrei Gromyko.

Mao mourut en 1976 ; sa femme et la « bande des Quatre » furent arrêtés. Le président Bhutto du Pakistan fut supplanté par le général Zia. Ian Smith perdit la guerre civile au Zimbabwe (ex-Rhodésie). Le président Allende fut tué au Chili par des rebelles soutenus par la CIA. Haïlé Sélassié, surnommé le « Lion de Judas », dut quitter l'Ethiopie en 1974. En Espagne, Franco mourut et Juan Carlos I monta sur le trône. Le shah s'enfuit d'Iran, de même que le général Amin d'Ouganda en 1979. En 1978, trois papes se succédèrent sur le trône pontifical.

En 1972, Edward Heath entama la procédure d'entrée de la Grande-Bretagne dans la Communauté économique européenne : De Gaulle n'était plus là pour dire « Non ! ». En 1977, Menahem Begin et le Likoud, son parti regroupant le centre et la droite, mirent fin à l'autorité britannique restée jusque-là intacte dans l'Etat d'Israël, fondé 29 ans plus tôt.

Jamais progressistes et agitateurs ne s'étaient autant démenés.

October 1972. With the cloud of the Watergate affair lowering over his head, Richard Nixon visits Ohio during his campaign to win a second term in the White House. He won by a landslide.

Oktober 1972. Die Watergate-Affäre schwebt zwar noch wie eine dunkle Wolke über seinem Kopf, doch Richard Nixon ist in Ohio bereits wieder auf Stimmenfang für eine zweite Amtsperiode im Weißen Haus. Er wurde mit überwältigender Mehrheit wiedergewählt.

Octobre 1972. Alors que les nuages menaçants du Watergate s'amoncellent sur sa tête, Richard Nixon fait une tournée en Ohio lors de la campagne électorale pour son second mandat à la Maison-Blanche. Il remporta une victoire écrasante.

Hail!... Gerald Ford takes the Presidential Oath of Office in the White House, 13 August 1974, with Chief Justice Warren Berger (right), and Betty Ford (centre). Ford was picking up the presidential pieces after the fiasco of Watergate.

Ich schwöre! ... Gerald Ford wird im Weißen Haus vom Obersten Richter Warren Berger (rechts) als Präsident vereidigt, 13. August 1974. Neben ihm steht seine Frau Betty (Mitte). Ford übernahm das „angeschlagene Präsidentenamt nach der Watergate-Affäre.

Je le jure ! ... Gerald Ford prête le serment présidentiel à la Maison-Blanche,13 août 1974. (A droite) le juge de la Cour suprême, Warren Berger, et Betty Ford (au milieu). Ford tentait de recoller les morceaux après le désastre du Watergate.

Farewell!... Richard Nixon gives an inappropriate thumbs-up sign after resigning from the presidency of the United States, August 1974. His son-in-law David Eisenhower is with him as he bids goodbye to White House staff.

Alles Okay! ... Richard Nixon nimmt mit einer unangemessenen Geste Abschied vom Präsidentschaftsamt der Vereinigten Staaten, August 1974. Sein Schwiegersohn David Eisenhower steht ihm bei seinem Abschied von den Mitarbeitern im Weißen Haus zur Seite.

Adieu ! ... Mal à propos, Richard Nixon fait signe que tout va bien après sa démission de la présidence des Etats-Unis, août 1974. Son gendre, David Eisenhower, l'accompagne alors qu'il fait ses adieux au personnel de la Maison-Blanche.

Gerald Ford (right) and Leonid
Brezhnev (left) toast each other
at a dinner in Vladivostok,
November 1974. They were
celebrating successful talks that
would 'constrain our military
competition over the next
decade'.

Gerald Ford (rechts) und
Leonid Breschnew (links) bei
einem Staatsessen in
Wladiwostok, November 1974.
Sie stoßen feierlich auf ihre
erfolgreichen Unterredungen
an, die „die Begrenzung des
Rüstungswettkampfs ihrer
beiden Länder im kommenden
Jahrzehnt" vorsahen.

Gerald Ford (à droite) et
Leonid Brejnev (à gauche) se
portent un toast lors d'un dîner
à Vladivostok, novembre 1974.
Ils fêtent les négociations
fructueuses censées « réduire
leur concurrence militaire lors
de la prochaine décennie ».

November 1973. Libyan leader Muammar al-Quaddafi (better known as Colonel Gaddafi) speaks to the press at a Paris hotel, after talks with President Pompidou.

November 1973. Der libysche Staatschef Muammar Kadhdhafi (besser bekannt als Oberst Gaddafi) auf einer Pressekonferenz, die er nach Gesprächen mit dem französischen Präsidenten Georges Pompidou in Paris gab.

Novembre 1973. Le leader libyen Muammar al-Kadhafi (plus connu sous le nom de colonel Kadhafi) donne une conférence de presse dans un hôtel parisien à la suite d'une rencontre avec le président Pompidou.

May 1973. Henry Kissinger, American
special envoy, leaves the Elysée Palace,
Paris, after discussing the Soviet Union
with President Pompidou.

Mai 1973. Der amerikanische Sonderbe-
auftragte Henry Kissinger verläßt nach
Gesprächen mit Präsident Pompidou über
die Sowjetunion den Pariser Elysée-Palast.

Mai 1973. Henry Kissinger, envoyé spécial
américain, sort du palais de l'Elysée à Paris
après des discussions sur l'Union soviétique
avec le président Pompidou.

Abdul Monein Rifal of Jordan (right), and Yasser Arafat, leader of the Palestine Liberation Organization, after signing their peace treaty, 14 July 1970.

Abdul Monein Rifal von Jordanien (rechts) und der PLO-Führer Jasir Arafat, nachdem sie ein gemeinsames Friedensabkommen unterzeichnet haben, 14. Juli 1970.

Abdul Monein Rifal de Jordanie (à droite) et Yasser Arafat, leader de l'Organisation de libération de la Palestine, après la signature de leur traité de paix, 14 juillet 1970.

March 1979.
President Jimmy
Carter of the United
States (left) and
Menachem Begin of
Israel meet in Tel
Aviv at the outset of
peace talks between
Israel and Egypt.

März 1979. US-
Präsident Jimmy
Carter (links) und
der israelische
Ministerpräsident
Menachem Begin
treffen sich in Tel
Aviv bei Friedens-
gesprächen zwischen
Israel und Ägypten.

Mars 1979. Jimmy
Carter, le président
des Etats-Unis
d'Amérique (à
gauche) et Menahem
Begin d'Israël se
rencontrent à
Tel-Aviv lors de
l'ouverture des
négociations de
paix entre Israël et
l'Egypte.

Last days of a 16-year exile. The Ayatollah
Ruholla Khomeini in the garden of his
headquarters at Pontchartrain, on the
outskirts of Paris, November 1978.
On 1 February the following year Khomeini
returned to Iran.

Die letzten Tage des 16 Jahre andauernden
Exils. Der Ayatollah Khomeini im Garten
seines Hauses in Pontchartrain vor den Toren
von Paris, November 1978. Am 1. Februar
des folgenden Jahres kehrte Khomeini in den
Iran zurück.

Les derniers jours d'un exil de 16 années.
L'ayatollah Ruholla Khomeiny dans le jardin
de son quartier général à Pontchartrain en
banlieue parisienne, novembre 1978.
Le 1er février de l'année suivante, Khomeiny
retournera en Iran.

Weighed down with medals, President Idi
Amin Dada of Uganda puts new fear into the
hearts of his followers at an outdoor rally in
1978. The following year, the dictator was
forced to flee into exile.

Präsident Idi Amin Dada von Uganda trägt
schwer am Gewicht seiner Orden. Auf einer
Kundgebung 1978 flößt er seinen Anhängern
noch einmal Furcht ein. Nur ein Jahr später
mußte der Diktator das Land verlassen.

En 1978, lors d'un rallye en plein air, le
président Idi Amin Dada d'Ouganda, surchargé
de médailles, passe un savon à ses partisans.
L'année suivante, il sera forcé de s'exiler.

Jean-Bédel Bokassa, President and Emperor of the Central African Republic, on his throne, Coronation Day, 4 December 1977. His crown contained 5,000 diamonds.

Jean-Bédel Bokassa, Präsident und Kaiser der Zentralafrikanischen Republik bei den Inthronisationsfeierlichkeiten, 4. Dezember 1977. Seine Krone ist mit 5.000 Diamanten besetzt.

Jean-Bédel Bokassa, président et empereur de la république centrafricaine, sur son trône, le jour de son couronnement, 4 décembre 1977. Sa couronne était incrustée de 5 000 diamants.

Mobutu Sese Seko, President of Zaire, in a television interview at the height of the civil war in 1977. In front of him are captured Portuguese and Soviet arms, forged American banknotes, and two prisoners from the breakaway region of Katanga (now Shaba).

Mobutu Sese Seko, Präsident von Zaire, während einer Fernsehansprache im Jahre 1977. Das Land steckt tief im Bürgerkrieg. Vor ihm liegen sichergestellte, portugiesische und sowjetische Waffen sowie gefälschte amerikanische Banknoten. Neben ihm kauern zwei Gefangene der abtrünnigen Region Katanga (dem heutigen Shaba).

Mobutu Sese Seko, président du Zaïre, lors d'une interview à la télévision en 1977, alors que la guerre civile bat son plein. Devant lui se trouvent des armes soviétiques et portugaises, ainsi que des dollars américains falsifiés et deux prisonniers de la région dissidente du Katanga (appelée aujourd'hui Shaba).

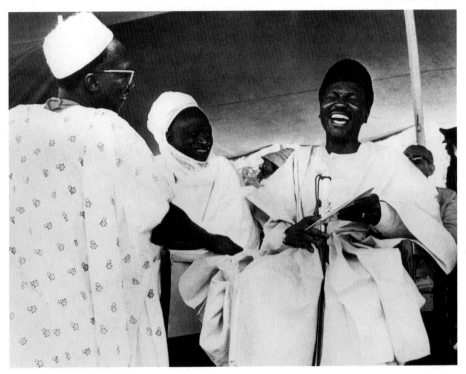

January 1970. General Yakubu Gowon of Nigeria (right) with friends at a polo match. Two weeks earlier, the province of Biafra had conceded defeat after a bitter war of two and a half years.

Januar 1970. General Yakubu Gowon von Nigeria (rechts) besucht mit Freunden ein Polo-Spiel. Zwei Wochen zuvor hatte sich die Provinz Biafra nach zweieinhalb Jahren erbitterter Kämpfe geschlagen gegeben.

Janvier 1970. Le général Yakubu Gowon du Niger (à droite) avec des amis lors d'un match de polo. Deux semaines plus tôt, la province du Biafra s'était rendue après une guerre cruelle qui dura deux ans et demi.

The body of Steve Biko, 25 October 1977. The South African political activist and founder of the Black Consciousness movement died as a result of the ferocious beatings he received while in police custody.

Der Leichnam von Steve Biko, 25. Oktober 1977. Der südafrikanische Aktivist und Gründer der Black-Consciousness-Bewegung war beim Verhör von der Polizei zu Tode geprügelt worden.

Le corps de Steve Biko, 25 octobre 1977. Militant politique sud-africain et fondateur du mouvement Black Consciousness, il mourut des suites des coups reçus en prison.

Piet Botha waves
to his supporters in
the South African
houses of parliament
after his election as
president in October
1978.

Piet Botha winkt
seinen Anhängern
im südafrikanischen
Abgeordnetenhaus
zu, nachdem er die
Präsidentschafts-
wahlen gewonnen
hatte, Oktober
1978.

Piet Botha salue ses
partisans du parle-
ment sud-africain
après son élection
à la présidence,
octobre 1978.

November 1971. Fidel Castro, Prime Minister of Cuba (left) and President Salvador Allende of Chile wave to crowds in Santiago. What Allende called 'the germs of fascism' were already at work to destroy his democratically elected government.

November 1971. Der kubanische Staatschef Fidel Castro (links) und der chilenische Präsident Salvador Allende zeigen sich in Santiago den Massen. Die „Keime des Faschismus", wie Allende sie nannte, waren zu jenem Zeitpunkt schon aktiv, um seine demokratisch gewählte Regierung zu stürzen.

Novembre 1971. Le Premier ministre cubain Fidel Castro (à gauche), et le président chilien Salvador Allende saluent les foules de Santiago. Ce qu'Allende appelait les « germes du fascisme » est déjà à l'œuvre pour renverser son gouvernement démocratique.

In the shadow of
Charles de Gaulle...
The French Prime
Minister Jacques
Chirac addresses an
assembly of the
Union démocratique
républicaine, 1975.

Im Schatten von
Charles de Gaulle ...
Der französische
Premierminister
Jacques Chirac
während einer Rede
auf dem Parteitag
der Union démo-
cratique républi-
caine, 1975.

Dans l'ombre de
Charles de Gaulle ...
Jacques Chirac, le
Premier ministre
français, s'adresse à
l'assemblée de
l'Union démo-
cratique républi-
caine, 1975.

In the shadow of
Konrad Adenauer...
Helmut Kohl
shortly after being
re-elected to the
national chair of the
German Christian
Democratic Union,
July 1975.

Im Schatten von
Konrad Adenauer ...
Der Christdemokrat
Helmut Kohl kurz
nach seiner Wieder-
wahl als Parteivor-
sitzender, Juli 1975.

Dans l'ombre de
Konrad Adenauer ...
Helmut Kohl, peu
de temps après sa
réélection à la
présidence de
l'Union chrétienne
démocrate, juillet
1975.

Zulfikar Ali Bhutto, President and Prime Minister of Pakistan,
March 1977. It was the year of his landslide election victory,
which was followed almost immediately by an Army coup. A year
later Bhutto was sentenced to death.

Der pakistanische Staatspräsident und Premierminister Zulfikar
Ali Bhutto, März 1977. Es war das Jahr seines überwältigenden
Wahlsiegs, auf den fast unmittelbar ein Militärputsch folgte. Ein
Jahr später wurde Bhutto zum Tode verurteilt.

Zulfikar Ali Bhutto, président et Premier ministre du Pakistan,
mars 1977. Ce fut l'année de son écrasante victoire électorale,
presque immédiatement suivie d'un coup d'Etat militaire. Un an
plus tard, il sera condamné à mort.

Chancellor Helmut
Schmidt of West
Germany at the
Bilderberg
Conference, April
1977. Schmidt
gained much
popularity with
his stand against
terrorism.

Bundeskanzler
Helmut Schmidt auf
der Konferenz von
Bilderberg, April
1977. Schmidt
hatte mit seinen
Maßnahmen gegen
den Terrorismus viel
Beifall geerntet.

Helmut Schmidt,
chancelier de la
RFA, lors de la
conférence de
Bilderberg, avril
1977. Ses positions
contre le terrorisme
le rendirent très
populaire.

Hear no evil, see no evil… Helmut Schmidt (left) and Margaret Thatcher,
Prime Minister of Britain, at a press conference at Millbank Tower, London,
11 May 1979. Thatcher's political reign was only eight days old.

Nichts Schlechtes hören, nichts Schlechtes sehen … Helmut Schmidt (links)
und Margaret Thatcher auf einer Pressekonferenz im Millbank Tower,
London, 11. Mai 1979. Thatchers Regentschaft war gerade erst acht Tage alt.

N'écoutez pas le mal, ne voyez pas le mal … Helmut Schmidt (à gauche) et
Margaret Thatcher, Premier ministre du Grande-Bretagne, lors d'une
conférence de presse à la Tour de Millbank, Londres, 11 mai 1979. Thatcher
ne régnait que depuis huit jours.

Think no evil, speak
no evil... Harold
Macmillan (left)
and Prime Minister
Edward Heath
of Britain negotiate
British entry into
Europe, Brussels,
January 1972.

Nichts Böses
denken, nichts Böses
sagen ... Harold
Macmillan (links)
und der britische
Premierminister
Edward Heath
verhandeln in
Brüssel über den
Beitritt Großbritan-
niens in die EU,
Januar 1972.

Ne pensez pas de
mal, ne dites pas de
mal ... Harold
Macmillan (à
gauche) et le
Premier ministre du
Grande-Bretagne,
Edward Heath,
négocient à
Bruxelles, l'entrée de
la Grande-Bretagne
dans l'Europe,
janvier 1972.

A grudging
reconciliation.
Queen Elizabeth II
and Wallis, Duchess
of Windsor, meet at
the funeral of
Edward, Duke
of Windsor, London,
5 June 1972.

Eine widerwillige
Aussöhnung. Köni-
gin Elizabeth II. von
England und Wallis,
die Herzogin von
Windsor, treffen sich
auf der Beerdigung
von Herzog Edward
von Windsor, Lon-
don, 5. Juni 1972.

Réconciliation
réticente. La reine
Elisabeth II et Wallis,
duchesse de Wind-
sor, se rencontrent
aux funérailles
d'Edward, duc de
Windsor, Londres,
5 juin 1972.

Margaret Thatcher, Secretary of State for Education and Science, tries on a new hat, 1971. She was nicknamed 'Milk-Snatcher' after she initiated legislation to put an end to free milk for schoolchildren.

Margaret Thatcher, Staatsministerin für Bildung und Wissenschaft, probiert einen neuen Hut, 1971. Nachdem sie per Gesetz für das Ende der Gratis-Milchvergabe an Schulkinder gesorgt hatte, erhielt sie den Spitznamen „Milk-Snatcher".

Margaret Thatcher, ministre de l'Education et de Sciences, essaye un nouveau chapeau, 1971. Elle fut surnommée « La kidnappeuse de lait » après avoir proposé une loi mettant fin à la distribution gratuite de lait dans les écoles.

Pope John Paul II (Karol Jozef Wojtyla), the first Polish pope and the first non-Italian pope for 450 years, kisses one of many tarmacs, 1979.

Papst Johannes Paul II. (Karol Jozef Woityla), der erste polnische Papst und der erste nichtitalienische Papst seit 450 Jahren küßt einen der zahlreichen Böden, auf dem er gerade gelandet ist, 1979.

Le Pape Jean-Paul II (Karol Jozef Wojtyla), premier Pape polonais ainsi que le premier, depuis 450 ans, à ne pas être Italien, embrasse le sol de l'un des nombreux aéroports où il vient d'atterrir, 1979.

December 1970. West German Chancellor Willy Brandt
kneels before the Polish National Memorial in Warsaw. The
following year, Brandt was awarded the Nobel Peace Prize.

Dezember 1970. Der deutsche Bundeskanzler Willy Brandt
kniet vor dem polnischen Nationalmahnmal in Warschau.
Im darauffolgenden Jahr erhielt der Politiker den Friedens-
nobelpreis.

Décembre 1970. Le chancelier d'Allemagne fédérale Willy
Brandt s'agenouille devant le monument à la mémoire des
victimes du nazisme de Varsovie. Il recevra le prix Nobel de
la paix l'année suivante.

May 1975. Deng Xiaoping, Deputy Prime Minister of China, at a press conference in Paris. The war in Vietnam had just ended.

Mai 1975. Der stellvertretende Ministerpräsident der Volksrepublik China Deng Xiaoping auf einer Pressekonferenz in Paris. Der Vietnamkrieg war gerade beendet worden.

Mai 1975. Deng Xiaoping, Premier ministre chinois, lors d'une conférence de presse à Paris. La guerre du Viêt-nam venait juste de se terminer.

'We intend to remain alive. Our neighbours want to see us dead. This is not a question that leaves much room for compromise.' Golda Meir, Prime Minister of Israel, 12 November 1972.

„Wir wollen am Leben bleiben. Unsere Nachbarn würden uns lieber tot sehen. Dies ist ein Konflikt, der nicht viel Handlungsspielraum läßt." Golda Meir, Ministerpräsidentin von Israel, 12. November 1972.

« Nous avons l'intention de rester vivants. Nos voisins désirent nous voir morts. Une chose est sûre, cela ne laisse pas beaucoup de place aux compromis. » Golda Meir, Premier ministre d'Israël, 12 novembre 1972.

2. Conflict
Konflikte
Les conflits

January 1973. A badly wounded South Vietnamese soldier. Half way round the world, peace negotiations were taking place in Paris, but the killing and maiming continued.

Januar 1973. Ein schwerverwundeter südvietnamesischer Soldat. Am anderen Ende der Welt fanden Friedensverhandlungen statt, doch das Töten und das Verstümmeln von Menschen nahm kein Ende.

Janvier 1973. Un soldat du Viêt-nam du Sud grièvement blessé. Pendant que tueries et mutilations se poursuivaient, on négociait la paix à Paris.

2. Conflict
Konflikte
Les conflits

Students of conflict had much to concern them during the Seventies. There were the age-old rivalries that had survived like ancient plagues – in Cyprus, where Greek and Turk sniped at each other for possession of the island, and in Northern Ireland, where sectarian violence was bitterly resurrected. There were wars that bled over from the Sixties – in Vietnam, Nigeria, Cambodia and Rhodesia/Zimbabwe. And there were dozens more wars, revolutions and risings that the Seventies managed to generate from scratch.

Before the decade was a year old, civil war broke out in East Pakistan, and seven million refugees shuffled to and fro across a subcontinent, seeking asylum in or escape from the newly created state of Bangladesh. Local wars blazed across political frontiers. The Rhodesian civil war spilled into Mozambique in 1977. The Vietnam war brought death and chaos to Laos and Cambodia. Revolutions broke out in Nicaragua, Afghanistan and Iran.

In the Lebanon, war began as a contest between Druze-Palestinian groups and Maronite Christians. Later it was to become impossibly complicated. In Angola the fight was trilateral, between the MPLA, supported by the USSR; the FNLA, backed by Zaire; and UNITA, backed by white South Africa, a murderous, repressive regime lucky to avoid its own civil war.

Den Konfliktforschern hatten die siebziger Jahre einiges zu bieten. Da gab es uralte Rivalitäten, die die Zeit wie eine Plage aus längst vergangenen Jahrhunderten überlebt hatten – in Zypern kämpften griechische und türkische Heckenschützen um die Vorherrschaft auf der Insel und in Nordirland zeigte sich die sektiererische Gewalt erneut von ihrer schlimmsten Seite. Einige der Kriege, die in den sechziger Jahren ausgebrochen waren, tobten in Vietnam, Nigeria, Kambodscha und Rhodesien (dem heutigen Simbabwe) weiter. Es gab noch ein Dutzend weiterer Kriege, Revolutionen und Aufstände, die in den Siebzigern aus dem Nichts entstanden.

Das erste Jahr der neuen Dekade war noch nicht vorüber, als in Ostpakistan ein Bürgerkrieg ausbrach. Sieben Millionen Flüchtlinge irrten auf dem Subkontinent herum; einige hofften in dem neugegründeten Staat Bangladesch Asyl zu finden, andere flohen aus diesem Land. Die Kriege breiteten sich über die nationalen Grenzen hinweg aus. Der Funke des Bürgerkrieges in Rhodesien sprang 1977 auf Mosambik über. Der Vietnamkrieg hinterließ blutige Spuren in Laos und Kambodscha. In Nicaragua, Afghanistan und im Iran brachen Revolutionen aus.

Im Libanon kam es zu Auseinandersetzungen zwischen palästinensischen Drusen und maronitischen Christen. Die Konfliktparteien waren so tief zerstritten, daß eine Lösung immer unwahrscheinlicher wurde. In Angola fanden Kämpfe zwischen drei politischen Gruppen statt, der von der UdSSR unterstützten MPLA, der von Zaire geförderten FNLA und der UNITA, der das mörderische und repressive Regime des Weißen Südafrikas den Rücken stärkte, um einen Bürgerkrieg im eigenen Land verhindern zu können.

Les observateurs des conflits furent très sollicités durant les années soixante-dix. De vieilles rivalités avaient survécu telles d'anciens fléaux – à Chypre, où Grecs et Turcs se battaient pour la possession de l'île, et en Irlande du Nord, où la violence sectaire reprenait ses droits. Certains conflits étaient hérités des années soixante – au Viêt-nam, au Niger, au Cambodge et au Zimbabwe (ex-Rhodésie). Mais les années soixante-dix virent surgir du néant des douzaines de guerres, révolutions et soulèvements en tous genres.

La décennie n'avait pas un an qu'une guerre civile éclata dans l'est du Pakistan et entraîna l'exode de sept millions de réfugiés à travers le sous-continent, qui demandaient asile à l'Etat du Bangladesh nouvellement créé ou cherchaient à en sortir. Des guerres locales se déclarèrent de part et d'autre des frontières politiques. La guerre civile rhodésienne s'étendit au Mozambique en 1977. La guerre du Viêt-nam attira mort et chaos sur le Laos et le Cambodge. Des révolutions éclatèrent au Nicaragua, en Afghanistan et en Iran.

Au Liban, la guerre commença par des combats entre Palestiniens druses et chrétiens maronites. Puis, la situation se compliqua à l'extrême. En Angola, la bataille était trilatérale, entre le MPLA, soutenu par l'URSS, le FNLA, appuyé par le Zaïre, et l'UNITA soutenue par l'Afrique du Sud blanche, gouvernement assassin et répressif qui évitait ainsi une guerre civile dans son propre pays.

A group of North Vietnamese prisoners captured in Cambodia, 1970.
They are blindfolded and labelled ready to be sent back across the border.
Nixon sent US troops into Cambodia in April 1970 as a 'necessary
extension of the Vietnam War'.

Eine in Kambodscha gefangengenommene Gruppe von Nordvietnamesen,
1970. Man hat ihnen die Augen verbunden und sie mit Zetteln
gekennzeichnet, um sie anschließend über die Grenze zurückzuschicken.
Nixon entsandte im April 1970 US-Truppen nach Kambodscha, eine „not-
wendige Ausweitung des Vietnamkrieges", wie es hieß.

Un groupe de prisonniers du Viêt-nam du Nord capturés au Cambodge,
1970. On leur a bandé les yeux et on les a étiquetés pour les renvoyer de
l'autre côté de la frontière. En avril 1970, Nixon envoya des troupes au
Cambodge, il était « nécessaire de prolonger la guerre du Viêt-nam ».

March 1970. A US
Marine carries an
elderly Vietnamese
woman to a
helicopter for
evacuation to a
refugee centre.

März 1970. Ein
US-Soldat trägt eine
alte vietnamesische
Frau zu einem Hub-
schrauber, der sie in
ein Flüchtlingslager
bringen soll.

Mars 1970. Un GI
américain transporte
une vieille femme
vietnamienne vers
un hélicoptère pour
l'évacuer vers un
centre de réfugiés.

March 1971. North Vietnamese troops attack a South Vietnamese
paratroop base in Laos. US and South Vietnamese troops poured into Laos
in an attempt to cut enemy supply lines down the Ho Chi Minh trail.

März 1971. Nordvietnamesische Truppen greifen eine südvietnamesische
Luftlandebasis in Laos an. US-Truppen und südvietnamesische Einheiten
drangen nach Laos vor, um den feindlichen Nachschub, der über den Ho-
Chi-Minh-Pfad gelangte, abzuschneiden.

Mars 1971. Des troupes nord-vietnamiennes attaquant une base de
parachutistes sud-vietnamiens au Laos. Les troupes américaines et sud-
vietnamiennes arrivèrent en masse au Laos pour tenter de couper les lignes
de ravitaillement ennemies le long de la piste Hô Chi Minh.

Vietcong troops
fighting in the
Quang Tri-Thua
Thien area of South
Vietnam, 1973.
US troops had
already left, but the
war had two more
years to run.

Vietcong-Einheiten
kämpfen in dem
Gebiet von Quang
Tri-Thua Thien in
Südvietnam, 1973.
Zwar hatten die US-
Truppen inzwischen
das Land verlassen,
doch der Krieg sollte
noch zwei weitere
Jahre dauern.

Troupes du Viêt-
cong combattant
dans le Quang Tri-
Thua Thien, région
du Viêt-nam du Sud,
1973. Les troupes
américaines se sont
déjà retirées, mais la
guerre durera encore
deux ans.

March 1973. Gavin Young's photograph of Vietnamese former prisoners of war leaping from their boats, as uniformed members of the Vietcong rush to meet them.

März 1973. Auf dem Foto von Gavin Young springen ehemalige vietnamesische Kriegsgefangene aus ihren Booten, als sie auf uniformierte Vietcong-Soldaten treffen.

Mars 1973. Photographie de Gavin Young montrant d'anciens prisonniers de guerre vietnamiens sautant de leurs bateaux, alors que des membres en uniforme du Viêt-cong se précipitent vers eux.

A young Khmer
Rouge soldier in
a street in Phnom
Penh, Cambodia,
16 May 1975. The
city had fallen to
communist forces
one month earlier…

Ein junger Soldat
der Roten Khmer
patroulliert in einer
Straße in Phnom
Penh, Kambodscha,
16. Mai 1975. Die
Stadt war einen
Monat zuvor in die
Hände der kommu-
nistischen Streit-
kräfte gefallen …

Un jeune soldat
khmer rouge dans
une rue de Phnom
Penh au Cambodge,
16 mai 1975. La
ville est tombée
entre les mains des
communistes un
mois plus tôt …

...But the fighting continued. Children, hit by fragments from a rocket explosion as they ran to help a fallen Cambodian soldier, are lifted on to a truck to be taken to a clinic for treatment.

... Doch die Kämpfe hielten an. Diese Kinder wurden von Bombensplittern getroffen, als sie einem gefallenen kambodschanischen Soldaten zu Hilfe eilen wollten. Sie werden auf den Laster gehoben und in ein Krankenhaus gebracht.

... Mais les combats continuent. Des enfants, blessés par l'explosion d'une fusée alors qu'ils voulaient aider un soldat cambodgien, sont emportés vers un camion pour être soignés dans une clinique.

May 1979. Pol Pot and other leaders of Democratic Kampuchea patrol an area of Cambodia not yet occupied by the Vietnamese. Pol Pot had come to power two years earlier – in that time he had been responsible for the death of two and a half million people.

Mai 1979. Pol Pot und andere Anführer der demokratischen Kampuchea patrouillieren ein Gebiet in Kambodscha, das die Vietnamesen noch nicht erobert hatten. Pol Pot war zwei Jahre zuvor an die Macht gekommen – seit dieser Zeit hatte er den Tod von zweieinhalb Millionen Menschen zu verantworten.

Mai 1979. Pol Pot et d'autres leaders du Kampuchéa démocratique patrouillent dans une région du Cambodge non encore occupée par les Vietnamiens. Pol Pot était arrivé au pouvoir deux ans auparavant – durant cette période, il fut responsable de la mort de deux millions et demi de personnes.

The killing fields, 1979. Cambodian civilians and Vietnamese soldiers open some of the mass graves of the victims of Pol Pot. Long after he had been ousted from power, he remained the most feared figure in Cambodia.

Die Massengräber, 1979. Kambodschanische Zivilisten und vietnamesische Soldaten stehen vor Massengräbern mit Opfern des Pol-Pot-Regimes. Noch lange nachdem seine Schreckensherrschaft beendet war, gehörte der Führer der Roten Khmer zu den gefürchtesten Personen in Kambodscha.

Champs de la mort, 1979. Des civils cambodgiens et des soldats vietnamiens ouvrent quelques-uns des charniers où furent jetées les victimes de Pol Pot. Bien après son éviction du pouvoir, il demeura le personnage le plus redouté du Cambodge.

A Khmer Rouge
refugee and her
baby, 1979, after the
worst atrocities of
Pol Pot's regime had
been committed.

Eine Rote Khmer-
Flüchtlingsfrau mit
ihrem Baby, 1979,
als die schlimmsten
Greueltaten des Pol-
Pot-Regimes bereits
geschehen waren.

Une réfugiée Khmer
Rouge et son bébé,
1979. Après les pires
atrocités effectuées
sous le régime Pol
Pot.

Bloody Sunday, Bogside, 30 January 1972. Ten thousand
residents of Derry (Londonderry) and their supporters had
marched in protest at the internment of several citizens without
charge or trial. As tempers flared, 13 civilians were killed by
British troops.

Blutiger Sonntag, Bogside, 30. Januar 1972. In Derry
(Londonderry) gingen Zehntausende auf die Straßen und
protestierten gegen die illegale Inhaftierung von mehreren
Bürgern. Als die Wogen des Protests immer höher schlugen,
wurden 13 Zivilisten von britischen Einsatztruppen erschossen.

Dimanche sanglant à Bogside, 30 janvier 1972. Dix mille
habitants du Derry (Londonderry) et leurs partisans manifestent
contre l'incarcération de plusieurs de leurs concitoyens sans
procès et sans motif d'inculpation. Quand la colère éclata,
13 civils furent tués par les troupes britanniques.

Derry, 30 January 1972. Father
Edward Daly gives the last rites
to one of the civilians killed on
Bloody Sunday.

Derry, 30. Januar 1972. Pater
Edward Daly erteilt einem der
am Blutigen Sonntag getöteten
Zivilisten den letzten Segen.

Derry, 30 janvier 1972. Le père
Edward Daly donne les derniers
sacrements à l'un des civils tués
lors du dimanche sanglant.

A Belfast teenager is arrested during the prolonged unrest that followed the
Orange Day marches. British troops had been brought in at the request of the
Northern Ireland government 'to prevent a total breakdown of law and order'.

Ein Jugendlicher aus Belfast wird während der anhaltenden Unruhen, die auf
den Marsch des Oranier-Ordens folgten, festgenommen. Die Regierung Nord-
irlands hatte die britischen Truppen zu Hilfe gerufen, um „den Zusammenbruch
von Recht und Ordnung zu verhindern".

A Belfast, un jeune est arrêté lors des troubles prolongés qui suivirent la
procession des Orangistes d'Irlande du Nord. Des troupes britanniques furent
envoyées à la demande du gouvernement d'Irlande du Nord afin « d'empêcher
la transgression totale de la loi et de l'ordre ».

Fighting in the Falls Road, Belfast, 10 July 1970. Five
Catholics were killed, 60 injured, and hundreds of houses
devastated after the British Army imposed a local curfew.

Blutige Auseinandersetzungen in der Falls Road, Belfast,
10. Juli 1970. Fünf Katholiken wurden getötet, 60
verwundet und Hunderte von Häusern zerstört, nachdem
die britische Armee eine Ausgangssperre verhängt hatte.

Combats à Belfast, Falls Road, 10 juillet 1970. Cinq
catholiques furent tués, 60 blessés et des centaines de
maisons dévastées avant que l'armée britannique
n'impose un couvre-feu.

British troops saturate an Irish housing estate, 4 July 1972. Northern Ireland remained in a state of turmoil and tension for months after the events of Bloody Sunday.

Britische Truppen durchkämmen irische Häuser, 4. Juli 1972. Noch Monate nach den Ereignissen des Blutigen Sonntags war die Lage in Nordirland angespannt.

Des troupes britanniques occupent un lotissement irlandais, 4 juillet 1972. L'Irlande du Nord demeura dans un état de trouble et de tension durant bien des mois après les événements du dimanche sanglant.

October 1971. Young petrol bombers on the streets of Derry, photographed by Fulvio Grimaldi. Petrol bombs and stones were the weapons of both indignation and terrorism, and it was often difficult to distinguish one from the other.

Oktober 1971. Junge Demonstranten in den Straßen von Derry, fotografiert von Fulvio Grimaldi. Benzinbomben und Steine waren die Waffen der Empörung und des Terrorismus, und oft genug waren die verschiedenen Beweggründe nicht zu unterscheiden.

Octobre 1971. Des jeunes gens lancent des cocktails Molotov dans les rues de Derry, photographiés par Fulvio Grimaldi. Les pierres et les cocktails Molotov ayant été à la fois les armes de l'indignation et du terrorisme, il était bien difficile de faire une distinction.

July 1970. Young men throwing stones at members of the Royal Ulster Constabulary (RUC) in the Falls Road, photographed by Malcolm Stroud. Trouble often flared in the summer, in the lead-up to the season of Orange Order marches.

Juli 1970. Auf dem Foto von Malcolm Stroud bewerfen junge Männer Mitglieder der RUC (Royal Ulster Constabulary) mit Steinen in der Falls Road. Die Unruhen brachen häufig im Sommer aus, wenn die alljährlichen Straßenmärsche des Oranier-Ordens bevorstanden.

Juillet 1970. Jeunes hommes jetant des pierres sur les membres du RUC (Royal Ulster Constabulary), Falls Road, photographiés par Malcolm Stroud. Des émeutes éclatèrent à maintes reprises cet été-là, précédant la période des processions orangistes.

Everyday life on the street. A Belfast woman
watches two armed British soldiers taking aim
outside her front door, 1970. The
photographer is David Newell Smith.

Alltägliches Straßenleben. Eine Frau in Belfast
beobachtet zwei britische Soldaten, die
unmittelbar neben ihrer Haustür ein Ziel
anvisieren, 1970. Der Fotograf ist David
Newell Smith.

Un jour comme les autres dans la rue. Une
femme de Belfast regarde deux soldats
britanniques armés, en position de mise en
joue, devant sa porte, 1970. Photographie de
David Newell Smith.

Firemen tend one
of over 150 victims
of an IRA car bomb
in Donegal Street,
Belfast, 21 March
1972. Six people
were killed.

Feuerwehrmänner
kümmern sich um
eins der 150 Opfer
bei einem Auto-
bomben-Anschlag
der IRA in der
Donegal Street,
Belfast, 21. März
1972. Sechs Men-
schen wurden ge-
tötet.

Des pompiers
soignent l'une des
quelque 150 vic-
times d'une bombe
déposée par l'IRA
dans une voiture,
Donegal Street,
Belfast, 21 mars
1972. Six personnes
furent tuées.

Mobilization Week, Teheran, February 1979.
Iranian women in traditional chadors march
past the US Embassy, red carnations in the
muzzles of their rifles. The Ayatollah's rule
was under way.

Die Woche der Mobilmachung in Teheran,
Februar 1979. Iranerinnen demonstrieren im
traditionellen Schador vor der US-Botschaft
der Hauptstadt. In den Gewehrläufen stecken
rote Nelken. Die Herrschaft des Ayatollahs
war in Gang.

Semaine de mobilisation à Téhéran, février
1979. Des femmes en tchador traditionnel
défilent devant l'ambassade américaine, des
œillets dans le canon de leurs fusils. La loi de
l'ayatollah était en marche.

Afghanistan, 1979. Islamic fundamentalist Mujaheddin standing on
the wreckage of a Soviet Sikorsky helicopter gunship they have
brought down. The photograph is by Arnaud de Wildenburg.

Afghanistan, 1979. Islamische Mudschaheddi-Fundamentalisten
stehen auf dem Wrack eines sowjetischen Sikorsky, einem
Kampfhubschrauber, den sie abgeschossen haben. Dieses Foto stammt
von Arnaud de Wildenburg.

Afghanistan, 1979. Des fondamentalistes islamiques moudjahiddins se
tenant devant les débris d'un hélicoptère soviétique Sikorsky qu'ils
viennent d'abattre. Photographie d'Arnaud de Wildenburg.

A Kurd fighter
inspects an
unexploded Iraqi
bomb, Kurdestan,
March 1971. Iraq
granted autonomy
to the Kurds in
1970, after nine
years of war.

Ein kurdischer
Kämpfer inspiziert
eine nicht gezündete
irakische Bombe,
Kurdistan, März
1971. Nach neun
Jahren Krieg, ge-
währte der Irak den
Kurden im Jahre
1970 Autonomie.

Un combattant
kurde inspecte une
bombe irakienne
qui n'a pas explosé,
Kurdistan, mars
1971. En 1970,
l'Irak accorda leur
autonomie aux
Kurdes après neuf
années de guerre.

29 October 1973. An Israeli soldier leads a file of Egyptian prisoners of
war from the Suez front. The Yom Kippur War had begun on 6 October,
when Israel was invaded by Egypt and Syria in a surprise attack.

29. Oktober 1973. Ägyptische Gefangene werden von einem israeli-
schen Soldat an der Suez-Front abgeführt. Der Jom-Kippur-Krieg war
am 6. Oktober ausgebrochen, nachdem ägyptische und syrische Einheiten in einem Überraschungsangriff auf israelisches Gebiet vorge-
drungen waren.

29 octobre 1973. Un soldat israélien conduit hors du front de Suez
une file de prisonniers de guerre égyptiens. La guerre du Kippour
commença le 6 octobre quand Israël fut envahi par l'Egypte et la Syrie
lors d'une attaque surprise.

A Skyhawk plane supports an Israeli infantry column during the battle for the Golan Heights, 9 October 1973. After the initial attack, Iraq, Morocco, Saudi Arabia and Jordan joined the war against Israel.

Eine israelische Infanteriestellung bekommt Unterstützung von einem Skyhawk-Flugzeug während der Kämpfe auf den Golan-Höhen, 9. Oktober 1973. Der Irak, Marokko, Saudi-Arabien und Jordanien traten bald in den Krieg gegen Israel ein.

Un avion Skyhawk assiste une colonne de l'infanterie israélienne pendant les combats sur le plateau du Golan, 9 octobre 1973. Après l'attaque initiale, l'Irak, le Maroc, l'Arabie Saoudite et la Jordanie se joignirent à la guerre contre Israël.

28 July 1974. A victim of the hostility between Greeks and
Turks in Cyprus. The overthrow of the government by Greek
Cypriot troops had led to a Turkish invasion of the northern
part of the island earlier that month.

28. Juli 1974. Ein Opfer der Feindseligkeiten zwischen
Griechen und Türken auf Zypern. Die Absetzung der
Regierung durch griechisch-zypriotische Truppen hatte kurz
vorher im selben Monat zum Einmarsch türkischer Truppen
im Nordteil der Insel geführt.

28 juillet 1974. A Chypre, une victime des hostilités entre les
Grecs et les Turcs. Le renversement du gouvernement par les
troupes grecques chypriotes avait provoqué l'invasion turque
du nord de l'île un peu plus tôt le même mois.

A Greek Cypriot National Guardsman runs for cover
under heavy machine-gun fire from the roof of the Ledra
Palace Hotel, Nicosia, July 1974. The photograph was
taken by Tony McGrath of *The Observer*.

Ein griechisch-zypriotischer Wachsoldat sucht Deckung vor
dem gegnerischen Maschinengewehrfeuer, das vom Dach
des Hotels Ledra Palace auf ihn gerichtet ist, Nikosia, Juli
1974. Tony McGrath von *The Observer* nahm dieses Foto
auf.

Sur le toit de l'hôtel Ledra Palace, un officier de la Garde
nationale chypriote grecque court se mettre à l'abri sous
des tirs de mitraillette, Nicosie, juillet 1974. Photographie
de Tony McGrath de *The Observer*.

Dacca, December 1971. During the war for
Bengali independence in East Pakistan
(Bangladesh), a line of Bengali collaborators
await summary execution at the hands of the
Mukti-Bahini.

Dacca, Dezember 1971. Während des
bengalischen Unabhängigkeitskrieges in
Ostpakistan (Bangladesch) erwarten
bengalische Kollaborateure ihre Exekution
durch die Mukti-Bahini.

Dacca, décembre 1971. Pendant la guerre
pour l'indépendance bengali dans l'est du
Pakistan (Bangladesch). Une file de collaborateurs bengalis attendent leur exécution
sommaire par les Mukti-Bahini.

General Abdul
Siddigui, a Mukti-
Bahini guerrilla
leader, bayonets
defenceless Bengali
collaborators, 1971.

General Abdul
Siddigui, der Gue-
rilla-Führer der
Mukti-Bahini, geht
mit dem Bajonett
auf wehrlose
bengalische
Kollaborateure los,
1971.

Le général Abdul
Siddigui, un leader
des guérilleros
Mukti-Bahini, passe
à la baïonnette des
collaborateurs
bengalis sans
défense, 1971.

October 1975. In the hell and confusion of
the streets of Beirut, members of the
Christian Phalangist group attack Islamo
Progressive fighters near the Hilton Hotel.
The war was only a month old, but was
escalating rapidly.

Oktober 1975. In der Hölle und der Ver-
wirrung in den Straßen Beiruts, greifen
Mitglieder der christlichen Phalangisten
Soldaten der Islamischen Progressiven Front
an, hier in der Nähe des Hotels Hilton. Der
Krieg war erst einen Monat vorher ausgebrochen, eskalierte aber rapide.

Octobre 1975. Dans l'enfer et la confusion
des rues de Beyrouth, des membres du
groupe chrétien phalangiste attaquent des
combattants islamo-progressistes près de
l'hôtel Hilton. Cette guerre, qui avait débuté
un mois auparavant, s'intensifia rapidement.

December 1975. A woman pleads for help for her wounded
husband in the Dekwan district of Beirut. In the early months
of the war, the Lebanese government was reluctant to use
force to separate the rival factions.

Dezember 1975. Im Beiruter Viertel Dekwan fleht eine Frau
um Hilfe für ihren verwundeten Mann. In den ersten
Kriegsmonaten zögerte die libanesische Regierung, die
rivalisierenden Fraktionen mit Gewalt zur Ordnung zu rufen.

Décembre 1975. Dans la circonscription Dekwan de
Beyrouth, une femme supplie qu'on aide son mari blessé.
Dans les tout premiers mois de la guerre, le gouvernement
libanais était peu disposé à utiliser la force pour séparer les
factions rivales.

12 August 1978. The remains of the Fakrami
building in Beirut after a bomb containing
200 kilos of dynamite exploded, killing over
200 people.

12. August 1978. Die Überreste des Fakrami-
Gebäudes in Beirut, nachdem dort eine
Bombe mit 200 kg Dynamit explodierte. Bei
dem Anschlag wurden über 200 Menschen
getötet.

12 août 1978. Décombres de l'immeuble
Fakrami à Beyrouth, après l'explosion d'une
bombe contenant 200 kilos de dynamite qui
tua plus de 200 personnes.

Cloethe Breytenbach's picture of UNITA guerrillas on parade during the civil war in Angola, 1976. After the hurried Portuguese withdrawal in 1975, fighting erupted as the FNLA and UNITA challenged the MPLA People's Government.

Die Fotografie von Cloethe Breytenbach zeigt eine Parade von Guerilla-Truppen der UNITA im angolanischen Bürgerkrieg, 1976. Nach dem übereilten Abzug der Portugiesen 1975 brachen Kämpfe aus, weil die FNLA und UNITA die Volksregierung der MPLA herausforderten.

Photographie de Cloethe Breytenbach représentant un défilé des guérilleros de l'UNITA pendant la guerre civile en Angola, 1976. Après le retrait hâtif des Portugais en 1975, des combats éclatèrent lorsque le FNLA et l'UNITA contestèrent le gouvernement du MPLA.

Child soldiers parade during the revolutionary
war against government troops in Southern
Sudan, March 1971. The war had already piled
the suffering of slaughter on the horrors of
famine for over seven years.

Kinder paradieren als Soldaten des
Revolutionskrieges gegen Regierungstruppen im
Südsudan, März 1971. Seit über sieben Jahren
vermehrte der Krieg die ohnehin schon grausame
Hungergreuel durch die Leiden der Massaker.

Des enfants soldats défilent pendant la guerre
révolutionnaire contre les troupes
gouvernementales du Soudan du Sud, mars 1971.
Pendant plus de 7 ans, cette guerre ajouta à la
famine des souffrances horribles engendrées par
les massacres.

The look of suffering. A woman's face registers shock after witnessing
the murder of South West African People's Organization troops by
UNITA forces in the Angolan civil war, 1977.

Der Ausdruck des Leidens. Dieser Frau steht der Schock ins Gesicht
geschrieben, nachdem sie mit ansehen mußte, wie UNITA-Einheiten
im angolanischen Bürgerkrieg Mitglieder der Südwestafrikanischen
Volksorganisation ermordeten, 1977.

L'expression de la souffrance. Le visage de cette femme témoigne du
choc qu'elle a reçu après avoir assisté au meurtre des troupes
de l'Organisation du peuple sud-ouest africain par les forces de
l'UNITA, lors de la guerre civile en Angola, 1977.

Uganda, February 1973. Tom Masaba, an ex-officer of the Ugandan army and alleged guerrilla fighter against Idi Amin, is prepared for execution in Mbale.

Uganda, Februar 1973. Tom Masaba, ein ehemaliger Offizier der ugandischen Armee und angeblicher Guerilla-Kämpfer gegen das Regime Idi Amins, wird in Mbale zur Exekution vorbereitet.

Ouganda, février 1973. Préparatifs pour l'exécution au Mbale de Tom Masaba, ancien officier de l'armée ougandaise et présumé guérillero contre Idi Amin.

Soweto, 21 June 1976. Residents of the township called for a boycott of the South African government's introduction of Afrikaans as the language of instruction in secondary schools. Prime Minister Vorster ordered the restoration of order 'at all costs'.

Soweto, 21. Juni 1976. Township-Einwohner riefen zum Boykott gegen die von der südafrikanischen Regierung geforderte Einführung von Afrikaans als offizielle Unter-richtssprache an höheren Schulen auf. Premierminister Vorster ordnete die Wieder-herstellung von Ruhe und Ordnung „um jeden Preis" an.

Soweto, 21 juin 1976. Des habitants de la ville appellent au boycott de la loi du gouvernement sud-africain sur l'introduction de l'Afrikaans comme langue officielle dans les écoles secondaires. Le Premier ministre Vorster ordonna le rétablissement de l'ordre « à tout prix ».

Soweto, the same day. Rioting broke out, and the violent response of the authorities led to more than 100 people being killed and over 1,000 more injured. The township was virtually destroyed.

Soweto, am selben Tag. Aufstände brachen aus, und die brutale Antwort der Staatsgewalt forderte 100 Menschenleben, mehr als 1.000 Menschen wurden verletzt. Die Stadt glich einem Schlachtfeld.

Soweto, le même jour. Des émeutes éclatent et la réponse violente des autorités provoqua la mort de plus de 100 personnes et fit plus de 1 000 blessés.

October 1979. A member of the BPR (Popular Revolutionary Bloc) in El Salvador wears a *Star Wars* storm-trooper mask to caricature government attitudes during a satirical demonstration.

Oktober 1979. Ein Anhänger der BPR (Revolutionärer Volksblock) trägt während einer Demonstration in El Salvador die Maske der Sturmtruppen aus dem *Krieg der Sterne*, um damit die Haltung der Regierung aufs Korn zu nehmen.

Octobre 1979. Un membre du BPK (Bloc révolutionnaire du peuple) à El Salvador lors d'une manifestation satirique. Il veut, à travers le masque de membre de troupes d'assaut de *La Guerre des Etoiles* qu'il porte, faire une caricature de l'attitude du gouvernement.

El Salvador, October 1979. A mother displays a photograph of her child, who disappeared during the military coup.

El Salvador, Oktober 1979. Eine Mutter stellt das Bild ihres Sohnes zur Schau, der während des Militärputsches verschwunden war.

El Salvador, octobre 1979. Une mère expose la photographie de son fils disparu pendant le coup d'Etat militaire.

November 1979. A row of corpses laid out in St Rosario church,
San Salvador. They were the bodies of men killed by police in
street fighting following anti-government demonstrations in the
capital of El Salvador.

November 1979. Leichen in der Kirche von St. Rosario in San
Salvador. Diese Menschen wurden von der Polizei in einer
Straßenschlacht getötet, die sich aus einer Demonstration gegen
die Regierung in der Hauptstadt von El Salvador entwickelt hatte.

Novembre 1979. Une rangée de corps étendus dans l'église de
Saint-Rosario, San Salvador. Ce sont les hommes tués par la police
lors des combats de rue qui suivirent les manifestations
antigouvernementales dans la capitale d'El Salvador.

Nicaragua, 20 July 1979. Sandinista rebels and their supporters gather in Managua, following their ousting of President Somoza.

Nicaragua, 20. Juli 1979. Nach der Absetzung von Präsident Somoza versammeln sich sandinistische Rebellen und ihre Anhänger in Managua.

Nicaragua, 20 juillet 1979. Des rebelles sandinistes et leurs supporters sont rassemblés à Managua, à la suite de l'évincement du président Somoza.

Former prisoners of the Somoza regime take over the gaols, Managua, Nicaragua, 20 July 1979. The gaols were then used to house supporters of the defeated junta.

Ehemalige Gefangene des Somoza-Regimes nehmen die Gefängnisse Managuas in ihre Gewalt, Nicaragua, 20. Juli 1979. Nun saßen die Anhänger der geschlagenen Junta in den Kerkern ein.

D'anciens prisonniers du régime de Somoza envahissent la prison de Managua au Nicaragua, 20 juillet 1979. Les prisons furent ensuite utilisées pour héberger la junte vaincue.

The last known photograph of President Salvador Allende of Chile (centre, wearing spectacles), Santiago, 11 September 1973. Within hours he was dead. Opponents claimed he committed suicide. Supporters said he was shot by police. With his death democracy came to an end in Chile.

Das letzte offizielle Foto des chilenischen Präsidenten Salvador Allende (Mitte, mit Brille), Santiago, 11. September 1973. Wenige Stunden später war er tot. Seine Gegner behaupteten, er habe Selbstmord begangen. Seine Anhänger sagten, er sei von der Polizei erschossen worden. Fest steht, daß mit seinem Tod die Demokratie in Chile zu Ende ging.

Dernière photographie connue du président du Chili, Salvador Allende (au centre, portant des lunettes), Santiago, 11 septembre 1973. Quelque heures plus tard, il était mort. Ses adversaires affirmèrent qu'il s'était suicidé, ses partisans qu'il avait été abattu par la police. Sa mort annonça la fin de la démocratie au Chili.

3. Terrorism
Terrorismus
Le terrorisme

Leila Khaled in a refugee camp in Beirut, 1975. An activist in the Palestine Liberation Organization, Khaled terrified and angered Western press and politicians with her audacity, but fascinated them with her good looks. Stories about her were legion, including one that she kept grenades in her underwear.

Leila Khaled in einem Beiruter Flüchtlingslager, 1975. Als Aktivistin der palästinensischen Befreiungsorganisation PLO versetzte sie die westlichen Medien und Politiker mit ihrer Kaltblütigkeit in Angst und Schrecken, faszinierte aber gleichzeitig als attraktive Frau. Es waren viele Gerüchte über sie im Umlauf, beispielsweise, daß sie Granaten in ihrer Unterwäsche mit sich trug.

Leila Khaled dans un camp de réfugiés à Beyrouth, 1975. Militante de l'Organisation de libération de la Palestine, elle terrifia et irrita la presse et les politiciens occidentaux par son audace, mais sa beauté les fascina. On racontait beaucoup d'histoires à son sujet, notamment qu'elle portait des grenades dans ses sous-vêtements.

3. Terrorism
Terrorismus
Le terrorisme

Terrorism tore into the Seventies in a whirlwind of explosive violence. Never before had modern tools of the trade been so easy to obtain. Never before had 'do-it-yourself' destruction been so simple to master.

The terrorists themselves, collectively or individually, became celebrities on the world stage, achieving the kind of legendary status of Dick Turpin or Billy the Kid. They included the Red Brigades in Italy, the Baader-Meinhof Gang in West Germany, Carlos the Jackal, the Palestinian Black September Group, the US Weathermen, the Symbionese Liberation Army and dozens more, blazing their way across the front pages of the world's press.

Airports and planes were much favoured targets – at Entebbe, Larnaca, New York and Tel Aviv. Many United States embassies were forced to develop siege mentalities. World leaders were guarded as never before. Even clubs and pubs were attacked.

The IRA exported terrorism from Northern Ireland to mainland Britain. In 1972 the Black September Group brought terror to the Olympic Village in Munich. In Washington DC, the Senate wing of the Capitol was damaged by a bomb in March 1971.

For a while, it seemed, nowhere was safe.

Der Terrorismus überzog die Welt in den siebziger Jahren mit einem Wirbelsturm der Gewalt. Nie zuvor konnten moderne Waffen im Handel so leicht beschafft werden. Nie zuvor war es so einfach, Bomben selbst herzustellen.

Einzeltäter oder terroristische Gruppierungen erlangten einen zweifelhaften Weltruf, der nur noch mit dem des legendären Dick Turpin oder Billy the Kid vergleichbar war. Ob nun die Roten Brigaden aus Italien, die Baader-Meinhof-Gruppe aus Deutschland, Carlos der Schakal, die Palästinenser-Gruppe Schwarzer September, die US-Weathermen, die Symbionese Liberation Army, und dutzende andere – sie alle bahnten sich den Weg auf die Titelseiten der Weltpresse.

Flughäfen und Flugzeuge waren beliebte Ziele für Terrorakte – Entebbe, Larnaca, New York und Tel Aviv. Viele US-Botschaften waren gezwungen, sich auf eine Art geistigen Belagerungszustand einzurichten. Das Sicherheitsaufgebot für führende Politiker war so hoch wie nie zuvor. Sogar Nachtclubs und Kneipen wurden zur Zielscheibe von Anschlägen.

Die IRA dehnte ihre Terroraktionen von Nordirland auf das britische Festland aus. Bei den Olympischen Spielen 1972 in München verübte die Gruppe Schwarzer September einen blutigen Anschlag im Olympiadorf. In Washington D.C. wurde im März 1971 der Senatsflügel des Kapitols durch einen Sprengsatz beschädigt.

Eine Zeitlang sah es so aus, als gäbe es keinen sicheren Ort mehr auf der Welt.

Le terrorisme fit irruption dans les années soixante-dix dans une tornade de violence explosive. Jamais encore il n'avait été aussi facile de se procurer des armes modernes. Jamais encore des moyens de destruction n'avaient été aussi simples à fabriquer.

Les terroristes eux-mêmes, tant sur le plan collectif qu'individuel, devinrent des célébrités sur la scène internationale, acquérant le statut légendaire d'un Dick Turpin ou d'un Billy the Kid. Les Brigades rouges en Italie, la « bande Baader-Meinhof » en RFA, Carlos le Chacal, le groupe palestinien Septembre noir, les Weathermen américains, l'« armée symbionèse de libération » ainsi que des douzaines d'autres embrasèrent les titres de la presse mondiale.

Les aéroports et les avions furent les cibles préférées des commandos – Entebbe, Larnaka, New York et Tel-Aviv. Beaucoup d'ambassades américaines se virent forcées d'adopter une mentalité d'assiégés. Les grands de la planète étaient plus protégés que jamais. Même des clubs et des bars furent attaqués.

L'IRA exporta le terrorisme de l'Irlande du Nord vers le continent anglais. En 1972, le groupe Septembre noir terrorisa le village olympique de Munich. A Washington D.C., dans le Capitole, l'aile du Sénat fut endommagée par une bombe en mars 1971.

Durant ces années, on eut l'impression de ne plus être en sécurité nulle part.

Dawson's Field, North Jordan,
14 September 1970. Palestinian gunmen
destroyed five civilian planes, among them
a BOAC DC-10 and a Swissair DC-8.
The 50 hostages they had taken were
released before the explosions.

Dawson-Felder, Nordjordanien,
14. September 1970. Palästinenser
zerstörten fünf Zivilflugzeuge, darunter
eine BOAC DC-10 und eine DC-8 der
Swissair. Sie hatten 50 Geiseln genommen,
die sie vor der Sprengung der Flugzeuge
freiließen.

Dawson's Field, nord de la Jordanie,
14 septembre 1970. Des artilleurs
palestiniens détruisirent cinq avions civils,
parmi lesquels un DC-10 de la BOAC et
un DC-8 de la Swissair. Les 50 otages
furent relâchés avant les explosions.

San Francisco,
19 September 1975.
American heiress
Patty Hearst is
caught on a bank
surveillance camera
during a raid by the
Symbionese
Liberation Army.

San Francisco,
19. September 1975.
Die amerikanische
Millionenerbin Patty
Hearst während
eines Banküberfalls
der Symbionese
Liberation Army,
aufgezeichnet
von einer Über-
wachungskamera.

San Francisco,
19 septembre 1975.
L'héritière améri-
caine Patty Hearst
filmée par la caméra
de surveillance d'une
banque lors d'un
raid de l'« armée
symbionèse de
libération ».

June 1979. The
notorious Carlos the
Jackal. Carlos is
regarded by many as
the founder of late
20th-century
terrorism.

Juni 1979. Der be-
rüchtigte Terrorist,
Carlos der Schakal.
Viele halten ihn für
den Begründer der
Terrorwelle des
späten 20. Jahr-
hunderts.

Juin 1979. Le
fameux terroriste
Carlos le Chacal.
Beaucoup pensent
qu'il fut le fondateur
du terrorisme de la
fin du XXe siècle.

Andreas Baader, co-leader of the Baader-Meinhof Gang, January 1972. Baader was arrested after a series of bomb attacks on German cities.

Andreas Baader, Mitbegründer der Baader-Meinhof-Gruppe, Januar 1972. Er wurde nach einer Reihe von Bombenanschlägen in deutschen Städten gefaßt.

Andreas Baader, l'un des leaders de la bande Baader-Meinhof, janvier 1972. Il fut arrêté après une série d'attaques à la bombe contre des villes allemandes.

Ulrike Meinhof,
shortly after her
arrest, 19 June 1972.
She was sentenced
to eight years'
imprisonment, but,
like Baader, she
committed suicide
in gaol.

Ulrike Meinhof,
kurz nach ihrer
Verhaftung,
19. Juni 1972.
Sie wurde zu acht
Jahren Freiheits-
strafe verurteilt,
beging jedoch,
genauso wie Baader,
im Gefängnis
Selbstmord.

Ulrike Meinhof,
peu après son
arrestation,
19 juin 1972. Elle
fut condamnée à
huit ans de prison,
mais, tout comme
Baader, elle se
suicida, dans sa
cellule.

Hanns-Martin Schleyer, president of the Federal Association of German Industry and victim of the Baader-Meinhof Gang, September 1977.

Hanns-Martin Schleyer, Arbeitgeberpräsident und Opfer der Baader-Meinhof-Gruppe, September 1977.

Hanns-Martin Schleyer, président de l'Association fédérale de l'industrie allemande et victime de la bande Baader-Meinhof, septembre 1977.

Aldo Moro, Prime Minister of Italy and victim of the Red Brigades, March 1978. The picture was taken while he was being held hostage.

Aldo Moro, italienischer Ministerpräsident und Opfer der Roten Brigaden, März 1978. Das Foto wurde während seiner Entführung aufgenommen.

Aldo Moro, Premier ministre italien et victime des Brigades rouges, mars 1978. Cette photo fut prise alors qu'il était tenu en otage.

16 May 1978. Italian police cluster around the body of Aldo Moro, dumped in the boot of a car on the Via Caetani, Rome. The Red Brigades had threatened to kill Moro unless left-wing prisoners were released. No deal was made, and Moro was shot.

16. Mai 1978. Italienische Polizisten drängen sich um den Leichnam Aldo Moros im Kofferraum eines Wagens in der Via Caetani, Rom. Die Roten Brigaden hatten mit der Ermordung des Politikers gedroht, um die Freigabe inhaftierter Gesinnungsgenossen zu erzwingen. Der Handel fand nicht statt, und Moro wurde erschossen.

16 mai 1978. Des policiers italiens sont rassemblés autour du corps d'Aldo Moro, déposé dans le coffre d'une voiture sur la Via Caetani, Rome. Les Brigades rouges avaient menacé de tuer Moro si l'on ne relâchait pas des prisonniers communistes. Le marché ne fut pas conclu et Moro fut assassiné.

December 1975.
A woman hostage
from the Indonesian
Consulate in
Amsterdam. She and
others were held by
terrorists bargaining
for South Moluccan
independence.

Dezember 1975.
Eine weibliche Gei-
sel vor der indone-
sischen Botschaft in
Amsterdam. Sie und
andere wurden von
Terroristen gefan-
gengehalten, denen
es um die Unab-
hängigkeit der Süd-
molukken ging.

Décembre 1975.
Un otage féminin au
consulat indonésien
d'Amsterdam. Elle
fait partie des per-
sonnes prises en
otage par des ter-
roristes voulant
négocier l'indépen-
dance du sud des
Moluques.

A Black September terrorist in the Olympic Village, Munich, September 1972. Eleven members of the Israeli athletics team were murdered.

Ein Terrorist der Gruppe Schwarzer September im Münchner Olympia-dorf, September 1972. Elf israelische Sportler kamen bei dem Anschlag ums Leben.

Un terroriste de l'organisation clandestine Septembre noir au village olympique Munich, septembre 1972. Onze membres de l'équipe athlétique israélienne furent assassinés.

The wreckage of the Mulberry Bush public house in Birmingham,
England, after it had been destroyed by a Provisional IRA bomb,
22 November 1974. 21 people were killed and 182 injured in one of
the IRA's worst atrocities.

Der Pub Mulberry Bush im englischen Birmingham liegt in Schutt und
Asche, nachdem die IRA dort einen Sprengsatz gezündet hatte,
22. November 1974. Der Anschlag gehörte zu den blutigsten, die von
der IRA verübt wurden und forderte 21 Todesopfer und 182 Verletzte.

Les décombres du bistrot Mulberry Bush à Birmingham en Angleterre,
après sa destruction par une bombe de l'IRA, 22 novembre 1974.
21 personnes furent tuées et 182 blessées au cours d'un des attentats
les plus atroces de l'IRA.

5 October 1974.
A survivor is helped
from the Horse and
Groom, Guildford,
following another
IRA explosion which
killed four British
soldiers.

5. Oktober 1974.
Ein Überlebender
wird gestützt. Dieser
weitere Anschlag
der IRA in dem Pub
Horse and Groom in
Guildford forderte
das Leben von vier
britischen Soldaten.

5 octobre 1974.
On aide un survivant
à sortir du bistrot
Horse and Groom,
Guildford, à la suite
d'un autre attentat
de l'IRA qui provo-
qua la mort de
quatre soldats
britanniques.

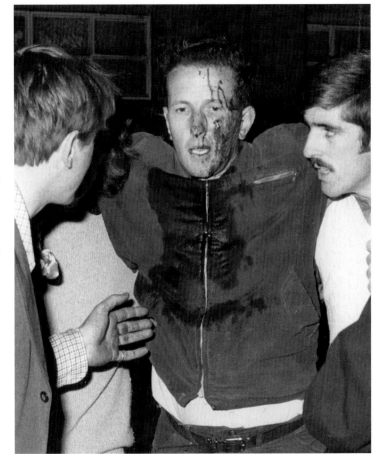

In 1978, three terrorists took hostages from the Iraqi Embassy in Paris. Subsequently, one terrorist was captured, one escaped, one (left) was killed.

1978 nahmen drei Terroristen in der irakischen Botschaft von Paris mehrere Geiseln. Später wurde einer der Terroristen gefaßt, einem gelang die Flucht, der dritte (links) wurde getötet.

En 1978, trois terroristes prirent en otage des membres de l'ambassade irakienne à Paris. Un terroriste fut capturé, le deuxième réussit à s'échapper et le troisième (à gauche) fut tué.

The hostages are snatched off the street outside the Embassy,
2 August 1978. France and Iraq had a 'special' relationship during
the Seventies, which included the sale of arms by the French – but
there was always tension and unease.

Die Geiseln mußten sich vor der Botschaft auf die Straße legen,
2. August 1978. Frankreich und der Irak hatten in den siebziger
Jahren ein „besonderes" Verhältnis zueinander, das auf dem
Waffenverkauf Frankreichs an den Irak beruhte – doch die
Spannungen und das Unbehagen hielten an.

Des terroristes s'emparent d'otages, dans la rue, devant l'ambassade,
2 août 1978. Dans les années soixante-dix, la France et l'Irak
entretinrent des relations « spéciales », basées sur la vente d'armes à
l'Irak par la France – mais tensions et malaises persistèrent.

4. Issues
Die großen Themen
Les grands thèmes

A member of the extreme right-wing and racist political group known as the British Movement is arrested by police in London, 1975. In the unrest of the Seventies, neo-fascism attracted an ugly mixture of bullies and malcontents.

Ein Mitglied der rechtsextremen und rassistischen Gruppe British Movement wird von der Polizei festgenommen, London 1975. Während der Unruhen der siebziger Jahren zogen neofaschistische Gruppen zahlreiche Schläger und unzufriedene Bürger an.

Un membre du groupe raciste d'extrême-droite connu sous le nom de Mouvement britannique est arrêté par la police, Londres, 1975. Pendant la période agitée des années soixante-dix, le néo-fascisme attira un mélange répugnant de mécontents et de brutes.

4. Issues
Die großen Themen
Les grands thèmes

It seemed that everything in the Seventies became an 'issue'. People woke up one morning to find their planet had been polluted and their environment under massive threat. All of a sudden it mattered what you ate, poured into the sea, released into the air. It was wrong to cover the countryside with tarmac and concrete, to imprison chickens in cages and calves in crates, to burn rubbish. There was horror at the leakage of radioactive nuclear waste from the Three Mile Island power station in Pennsylvania, and at the seepage of nearly 250,000 tonnes of crude oil from the wreck of the *Amoco Cadiz* off the coast of Brittany.

This much was new, but many of the issues were old. Racism and religious bigotry raised their ugly, angry heads – in London, in South Africa, in Ethiopia, in Iran and in Northern Ireland. Labour disputes brought mountains of uncollected rubbish on to the streets of London in 1970 and 1979, and violence to the Grunwick factory in the same year.

Scottish fishermen didn't like the EEC quota system. Japanese students didn't like the terms of the treaty with the United States that restored Okinawa to Japanese control. Greek students wanted free elections. Gays and feminists didn't like the way they were being treated.

It was not an easy time.

Alles schien in den Siebzigern zum „Problem" zu werden. Die Menschen stellten eines morgens fest, daß die Umweltverschmutzung auf ihrem Planeten zu einer massiven Bedrohung geworden war. Es wurde wichtig, was man aß, ins Meer leitete und in die Atmosphäre ausstieß. Es war falsch, den Boden zu betonieren, Hühner in Käfigen und Kälber in Verschlägen zu halten oder Müll zu verbrennen. Die Freisetzung von Radioaktivität beim Störfall in Three Mile Island in Pennsylvania wie die fast 250.000 Tonnen Rohöl, die aus der leckgelaufenen *Amoco Cadiz* an der bretonischen Küste ins Meer sickerten, lösten Panik aus.

Umweltschutz war ein neues Problem, viele andere waren allerdings altbekannt – in London, Südafrika, Äthiopien, im Iran und in Nordirland zeigten sich Rassismus und religiöse Bigotterie von ihrer häßlichsten Seite. Während der Streikwellen der Jahre 1970 und 1979 häufte sich der nicht abtransportierte Müll in den Straßen Londons und in der Fabrik Grunwick kam es 1979 zu Gewalttätigkeiten.

Schottische Fischer protestierten gegen die von der EG festgelegten Fangquoten. Japanische Studenten lehnten den Vertrag mit den Vereinigten Staaten ab, der Okinawa an Japan zurückgab. Griechische Studenten forderten freie Wahlen. Homosexuelle und Feministinnen wollten ihre gesellschaftliche Diskriminierung nicht länger dulden.

Es war keine einfache Zeit.

Au cours des années soixante-dix, tout sembla devenir un « problème ». Les gens se réveillèrent un beau jour en s'apercevant que leur planète était polluée et leur environnement très menacé. On se soucia soudain de savoir ce qu'on mangeait, ce qu'on déversait dans la mer, ce qu'on laissait échapper dans l'air. Il ne fallait plus bétonner la campagne, emprisonner les poulets dans des cages et les veaux dans des caisses, brûler les ordures. Il y eut un vent de panique après les fuites nucléaires radioactives de la centrale de Three Mile Island en Pennsylvanie et la marée noire le long des côtes bretonnes provoquée par presque 250 000 tonnes de pétrole brut échappé de l'épave de l'*Amoco Cadiz*.

Si tout cela était nouveau, les autres problèmes remontaient à bien plus loin – à Londres, en Afrique du Sud, en Ethiopie, en Iran et en Irlande du Nord, le racisme et la bigoterie religieuse dévoilèrent leur hideux visage. En 1970 et 1979, des mouvements sociaux provoquèrent l'entassement de montagnes d'ordures dans les rues de Londres et déclenchèrent de violentes émeutes la même année à l'usine Grunwick.

Les pêcheurs écossais s'élevaient contre le système des quotas imposé par la CEE, les étudiants japonais rejetaient les termes du traité passé avec les Etats-Unis, qui rendait Okinawa au Japon. Les étudiants grecs réclamaient des élections libres, les homosexuels et les féministes n'acceptaient pas la façon dont on les traitait.

Ce ne fut pas une époque facile.

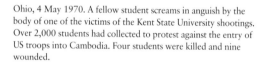

Ohio, 4 May 1970. A fellow student screams in anguish by the
body of one of the victims of the Kent State University shootings.
Over 2,000 students had collected to protest against the entry of
US troops into Cambodia. Four students were killed and nine
wounded.

Ohio, 4. Mai 1970. Eine Studentin schreit panisch auf, als einer
ihrer Kommilitonen auf dem Gelände der Universität von Kent
niedergeschossen wird. Über 2.000 Studenten hatten gegen den
Einmarsch der US-Truppen in Kambodscha protestiert. Vier
Studenten wurden bei der Kundgebung getötet, neun verletzt.

Ohio, 4 mai 1970. Une étudiante hurle sa colère auprès du corps
de l'une des victimes des tueries de l'université de Kent. Plus de
2 000 étudiants s'étaient rassemblés pour protester contre l'entrée
des troupes américaines au Cambodge. Quatre étudiants furent
tués et neuf blessés.

A Vietnam veteran in the Mall, Washington DC, 26 April 1971. In a series of
demonstrations to force US withdrawal from Vietnam, over 200,000 people gathered in the
capital. Veterans threw away their medals and carried placards reading 'Enough – out now'.

Ein Vietnam-Veteran in der Mall, Washington D.C., 26. April 1971. In einer Serie von
Demonstrationen versammelten sich über 200.000 Menschen in der Hauptstadt, um den
Rückzug der US-Streitkräfte aus Vietnam zu fordern. Kriegsveteranen warfen demonstrativ
ihre Orden weg und trugen Plakate mit der Aufschrift: „Genug – raus jetzt".

Un vétéran de la guerre du Viêt-nam, dans le Mall, Washington D.C., 26 avril 1971. Dans
le cadre d'une série de manifestations réclamant le retrait des forces américaines du Viêtnam,
plus de 200 000 personnes se rassemblèrent dans la capitale. Les vétérans avaient jeté leurs
médailles et portaient des pancartes indiquant : « Ça suffit – dehors maintenant ».

London, 10 May 1970. Vanessa Redgrave (centre, left) and Madame Lin Qui (centre, right) lead an anti-war demonstration to the American Embassy.

London, 10. Mai 1970. Vanessa Redgrave (Mitte, links) und Madame Lin Qui (Mitte, rechts) führen eine Anti-Kriegsdemonstration an. Der Marsch führt zur US-Botschaft.

Londres, 10 mai 1970. Vanessa Redgrave (au centre, à gauche) et Madame Lin Qui (au centre, à droite) marchent en tête d'une manifestation pacifiste se dirigeant vers l'ambassade des Etats-Unis.

New York, 1970. 'Battling Bella' Abzug, a lawyer who made her name
defending many of those accused of un-American activities, demands liberation
for women. Abzug was a political fighter who was later elected to Congress.

New York, 1970. Die Anwältin, „Battling Bella" Abzug, die berühmt wurde,
da viele ihrer Mandanten wegen anti-amerikanischer Aktionen angeklagt
waren, tritt für die Rechte der Frauen ein. Abzug war eine politische
Aktivistin, die später in den Kongreß gewählt wurde.

New York, 1970. « Battling Bella » Abzug, une avocate qui se rendit
célèbre en défendant des citoyens accusés d'activité anti-américaine,
revendique la libération des femmes. Abzug, farouche militante, qui fut
plus tard élue au Congrès.

'Screaming Lord Sutch'. The English pop star leads five naked women along a London street to publicize a rock festival at Wembley Stadium, 30 June 1972. The group were later arrested.

„Screaming Lord Sutch". Der englische Popstar zog mit fünf nackten Frauen durch eine Londoner Straße, um auf diese Weise für ein Rockfestival im Wembley-Stadion zu werben, 30. Juni 1972. Wenig später wurde die Gruppe festgenommen.

« Screaming Lord Sutch ». La pop star anglaise accompagne cinq femmes nues dans une rue de Londres pour faire de la publicité pour un festival de rock au stade de Wembley, 30 juin 1972. Le groupe fut arrêté peu de temps après.

July 1979. The Reverend John Kuiper (right) and his partner Roger Hooverman at a gay rights march on Fifth Avenue, New York. The pair were the first gay couple to be given the right to adopt a child.

Juli 1979. Der Pfarrer John Kuiper (rechts) und sein Freund Roger Hooverman nehmen an einem Protestmarsch der Schwulen und Lesben auf der Fifth Avenue in New York teil. Sie waren das erste homosexuelle Paar, dem die Adoption eines Kindes gewährt wurde.

Juillet 1979. Le révérend John Kuiper (à droite) et son partenaire Roger Hooverman lors d'une manifestation pour les droits des homosexuels sur la cinquième avenue de New York. Ce fut le premier couple homosexuel à obtenir le droit d'adopter un enfant.

Hold your placards high… One of the participators in a Gay Liberation Front protest in London, February 1971.

Haltet die Plakate hoch … Eine Teil-nehmerin auf der Protestkundgebung der Gay Liberation Front in London, Februar 1971.

Brandissez vos pancartes … L'une des participantes à la manifestation du Front de libération homosexuel à Londres, février 1971.

London, March 1970. The youngest MP in Britain, Bernadette Devlin, campaigns for civil rights in Northern Ireland on the steps of 10 Downing Street.

London, März 1970. Das jüngste britische Parlamentsmitglied Bernadette Devlin protestiert auf den Stufen von Downing Street 10 für die Bürgerrechte in Nordirland.

Londres, mars 1970. Le plus jeune membre du parlement britannique, Bernadette Devlin, fait campagne pour les droits civils de l'Irlande du Nord sur les marches du 10 Downing Street.

Northern Ireland, January 1979. The interior of a cell in the Maze Prison. It had been occupied by one of the 350 IRA prisoners who refused to wear prison clothes or to wash, and who smeared the walls of their cells with their own excrement.

Nordirland, Januar 1979. Das Interieur einer Zelle des Gefängnisses von Maze. Hier saß einer von 350 IRA-Gefangenen ein, die sich weigerten, Häftlingskleidung zu tragen und sich zu waschen, und die die Wände ihrer Zelle mit den eigenen Exkrementen beschmierten.

Irlande du Nord, janvier 1979. Intérieur d'une cellule de la prison Maze. Elle fut occupée par l'un des 350 prisonniers de l'IRA qui refusèrent de porter l'uniforme des détenus ou de se laver et qui souillèrent les murs de leur cellule de leurs propres excréments.

Rioting flares at the Notting Hill Carnival, 31 August 1976. Despite the drawn truncheons, the police are here retreating along the Portobello Road.

Straßenkämpfe beim Karneval in Notting Hill, 31. August 1976. Ungeachtet der gezogenen Gummiknüppel muß die Polizei ihren Rückzug entlang der Portobello Road antreten.

Des émeutes éclatent pendant le carnaval de Notting Hill, 31 août 1976. Malgré leurs matraques brandies, les policiers sont en train de battre en retraite le long de Portobello Road.

August 1972.
An Anglo-Asian
immigrant in
Downing Street
proclaims his
British citizenship.
He was one of
many refugees from
the Idi Amin regime
in Uganda.

August 1972. Ein
anglo-asiatischer
Einwanderer
proklamiert in der
Downing Street
seine britische
Staatsbürgerschaft.
Er war einer der
vielen Flüchtlinge
vor dem Regime Idi
Amins in Uganda.

Août 1972. Sur
Downing Street, un
immigrant anglo-
asiatique proclame
sa citoyenneté
britannique. C'était
l'un des nombreux
réfugiés du régime
de l'Idi Amine en
Ouganda.

A dejected picture
of white supremacy.
A skinhead member
of the British
Movement marches
through London,
1979.

Ein trauriges Bild
weißer Überlegen-
heit. Ein Skinhead
und Anhänger der
rechtextremen
British Movement
marschiert durch
London, 1979.

Image déprimante
de la suprématie
blanche. Un skin-
head, membre du
Mouvement britan-
nique, manifeste à
Londres, 1979.

Supporters of the racist views of the British MP Enoch Powell on an anti-Asian demonstration, 1972. Powell frequently spoke against black immigration to Britain, prophesying doom and 'rivers of blood' as the likely outcome.

Anhänger der rassistischen Parolen des britischen Parlamentsabgeordneten Enoch Powell auf einer anti-asiatischen Kundgebung, 1972. Powell machte des öfteren Front gegen die Immigration von Schwarzen, wobei er Verderben und „Sturzbäche von Blut" prophezeite.

Des supporters des idées racistes de Enoch Powell, membre du Parlement britannique, lors d'une manifestation anti-asiatique, 1972. Powell discourait souvent contre l'immigration noire, prophétisant ruine et « rivières de sang ».

Black and Asian Britons on the march from Hyde Park to
Downing Street, London, 21 March 1971. The march had
been organized by the Black People's Alliance against the
Conservative government's immigration bill.

Schwarze und asistische Briten auf einem Protestmarsch vom
Hyde Park zur Downing Street in London, 21. März 1971.
Die Demonstration war von der Black People's Alliance
organisiert worden gegen einen Gesetzesentwurf zur
Einwanderungsbeschränkung der Konservativen Regierung.

Des Britanniques noirs et asiatiques lors d'une manifestation
allant de Hyde Park à Downing Street, Londres, 21 mars
1971. Cette manifestation fut organisée par l'Alliance du
peuple noir contre le projet de loi sur l'immigration du
gouvernement conservateur.

13 August 1977.
John Hodder's
picture of fellow
photographers
surrounding police
as they make an
arrest during an
extreme right-wing
National Front
march.

13. August 1977.
Diese Fotografie von
John Hodder zeigt
eine von
Reporterkollegen
umringte Gruppe
von Polizisten, die
während eines
Protestmarsches der
rechtsextremen
Nationalen Front
eine Verhaftung
vornehmen.

13 août 1977. Une
photographie de
John Hodder
représentant ses
collègues entourant
la police lors d'une
arrestation au cours
d'une manifestation
du Front national
d'extrême-droite.

Anti-fascists burn the sign outside Robert Relf's house, Southall, July 1976. The sign read: 'For sale to an english family'.

Antifaschisten verbrennen ein Schild, das vor dem Haus von Robert Relf angebracht worden war, Southall, Juli 1976. Auf dem Schild stand: „Zum Verkauf an eine englische Familie".

Des antifascistes brûlent la pancarte placée devant la maison de Robert Relf, Southall, juillet 1976. Elle indiquait : « A vendre à une famille anglaise ».

A student response to the National Front
presence at a demonstration in London,
September 1974. The Front seldom provoked
enlightened discussion of their racist policies.

Die Antwort der Studenten auf Kampagnen
der Nationalen Front bei einer Demonstration
in London, September 1974. Nur selten regte
die Front zu einer erhellenden Diskussion
ihrer rassistischen Politik an.

Réponse des étudiants à la présence du Front
national au cours d'une manifestation à
Londres, septembre 1974. La politique raciste
du Front suscita peu de discussions éclairées.

Supporters of ZANU (the Zimbabwe African National Union)
demonstrate against the Rhodesian Conference in London,
11 September 1979. They were opposed to any deal with Ian Smith,
the white Prime Minister of Rhodesia. One sign reads 'Wanted for
murder – Ian Smith'.

Anhänger der ZANU (Simbabwes afrikanisch-nationale Union)
demonstrieren gegen die Rhodesien-Konferenz in London,
11. September 1979. Sie protestierten gegen jede Art neuer
Abkommen mit dem weißen Premierminister Rhodesiens Ian Smith.
Auf einem Plakat war zu lesen: „Als Mörder gesucht – Ian Smith".

Des supporters du ZANU (Union africaine nationale du Zimbabwe)
manifestent contre la Conférence rhodésienne, Londres, 11 septembre
1979. Ils étaient contre toute négociation avec Ian Smith, le Premier
ministre blanc de la Rhodésie. Une pancarte indique : « Recherché
pour meurtre – Ian Smith ».

Rhodesia, 1973. Crowds in a street greet Queen Elizabeth II on a royal visit. White Rhodesians, though desperately loyal to the British crown, could not accept the British government's opposition to their unilateral declaration of independence.

Rhodesien, 1973. Die Menschenmenge begrüßt Königin Elizabeth II. bei ihrem Staatsbesuch. Die weiße Regierung Rhodesiens konnte, obwohl sie verzweifelt Loyalität zur britischen Krone übte, den Widerstand der britischen Regierung gegen ihre einseitige Unabhängigkeitserklärung nicht akzeptieren.

Rhodésie, 1973. Dans la rue, la foule salue la reine Elisabeth II lors d'une visite royale. Les Rhodésiens blancs, pourtant désespérément fidèles à la couronne britannique, ne pouvaient accepter l'opposition du gouvernement britannique à leur déclaration d'indépendance unilatérale.

July 1977. Police remove a protester from the picket line outside the Grunwick film-processing laboratory, Willesden, London. The strike was fiercely contended by both sides, and there were over 500 arrests.

Juli 1977. Polizisten führen einen Streikposten vor der Filmverarbeitungsfirma Grunwick ab, Willesden, London. Während des Streiks wurde auf beiden Seiten erbittert gekämpft, und es gab über 500 Festnahmen.

Juillet 1977. Des policiers éloignent un contestataire du piquet de grève devant les laboratoires cinématographiques de Grunwick, Willesden, Londres. Lors de cette grève, on lutta de façon acharnée des deux côtés et il y eut plus de 500 arrestations.

No one seems likely to argue with this picket at a depot near the Surrey Docks, East London, 1978. The picket was preventing 'blackleg' labour from entering a lorry park during a drivers' strike.

Mit diesem Streikposten auf einem Lagergelände nahe den Surrey Docks im Osten Londons, will sich bestimmt niemand anlegen, 1978. Der Posten verbietet „Streikbrechern" die Zufahrt auf das Fuhrparkgelände.

Personne ne semble être en mesure de discuter avec ce piquet de grève se tenant devant un dépôt près des docks de Surrey, est de Londres, 1978. Il empêchait les travailleurs « traîtres » d'entrer dans un parking pour poids lourds lors d'une grève des chauffeurs.

Japanese commuters walk to work during a strike by the Public Corporation Workers' Union, Tokyo, November 1975.

Japanische Pendler müssen während eines von der Arbeitergewerkschaft organisierten Streiks zu Fuß zur Arbeit gehen, Tokio, November 1975.

Des banlieusardes japonaises se rendent à pied à leur travail pendant une grève du syndicat Public Corporation Workers' Union, Tokyo, novembre 1975.

Almost exactly one year earlier, Japanese
'Bullet Trains' lie idle at Shingawa Railway
Station during a 24-hour transport strike,
November 1974.

Fast genau ein Jahr zuvor liegen
japanische „Kugelzüge" während eines
24stündigen Streiks im Transportwesen
auf den Gleisen des Shingawa-Bahnhofs
still, November 1974.

A peine un an plus tôt, des trains japonais
« Bullet », à l'arrêt en gare de Shingawa,
lors d'une grève des transports qui dura
24 heures, novembre 1974.

A nurse holds a baby in the maternity unit at St Andrew's Hospital, Dollis Hill, London, during an energy dispute, December 1970.

Eine Krankenschwester der Entbindungsstation des St. Andrew's Hospital in Dollis Hill hält ein Baby im Arm; die Stromversorger Londons befanden sich im Ausstand, Dezember 1970.

A la maternité de l'hôpital St. Andrew, Dollis Hill, Londres, une infirmière tient un bébé dans ses bras pendant une grève d'électricité, décembre 1970.

January 1974. Four women workers at the Slumberdown factory in London use their company's quilts to keep warm during power cuts in the 'Winter of Discontent'.

Januar 1974. Vier Mitarbeiterinnen der Fabrik Slumberdown in London wärmen sich mit den firmeneigenen Decken. In jenem „Winter der Unzufriedenheit" war die Energieversorgung knapp.

Janvier 1974. Quatre ouvrières de l'usine de Slumberdown à Londres utilisent des édredons fabriqués par leur société pour se tenir au chaud pendant les coupures de courant de « l'Hiver du mécontentement ».

Shepherd Street, Mayfair, February 1979.
As the decade began, so it ended with a strike
by London's refuse collectors. There were
rumours that London was about to be
plagued by rats, but no Pied Piper was
needed.

Shepherd Street, Mayfair, Februar 1979. Wie
das Jahrzehnt begonnen hatte, so endete es
auch mit einem Streik der Müllabfuhr. Es gab
Gerüchte, daß London von einer Rattenplage
bedroht sein würde, aber der Rattenfänger
wurde nicht gebraucht.

Shepherd Street, Mayfair, février 1979. La
décennie se termina comme elle avait commencé par une grève des éboueurs de
Londres. On racontait que Londres allait être
infestée par les rats, toutefois l'on se passa du
preneur de rats.

Protestors – many of them with their children – demonstrate against the growing world population, May 1973. This was at a time when the population of the USA had reached 205 million, that of the Soviet Union 250 million and, it was said, seven babies were born in Bangladesh every minute.

Demonstranten – viele mit ihren Kindern – protestieren gegen die Bevölkerungsexplosion auf der Welt, Mai 1973. Zu dieser Zeit hatten die USA 205 Millionen Einwohner, die Sowjetunion 250 Millionen, und es hieß, daß in Bangladesch jede Minute sieben Kinder auf die Welt kämen.

Des contestataires – dont beaucoup avec des enfants – manifestent contre l'accroissement de la population mondiale, mai 1973. A cette époque, la population des Etats-Unis atteignait 205 millions d'habitants, celle de l'Union soviétique 250 millions et l'on disait que sept bébés naissaient toutes les minutes au Bangladesh.

Friends of the Earth demonstrate against the wasting of
paper, County Hall, London, March 1974. Few people then
(as now) realized the importance of rationing and husbanding
the world's resources.

Umweltschützer protestieren gegen die Verschwendung von
Papier vor der County Hall in London, März 1974. Wenige
Menschen begriffen damals (wie heute), daß man mit den
Rohstoffreserven der Welt haushalten muß.

Les Amis de la Terre manifestent contre le gaspillage de
papier, County Hall, Londres, mars 1974. A l'époque (et
aujourd'hui encore), peu de personnes réalisaient
l'importance de rationner et ménager les ressources terrestres.

A seal covered in
oil is washed up on a
polluted beach
in Wales, 1975.

Eine vollkommen
mit Öl bedeckte
Robbe ist an den
verseuchten Strand
von Wales ange-
trieben worden,
1975.

Un phoque recou-
vert de pétrole rejeté
sur une plage pol-
luée de Pays des
Galles, 1975.

The wreck of the giant tanker *Amoco Cadiz* off the coast of Brittany, Northern France, 26 March 1978. More than 230,000 tonnes of crude oil polluted over 100 miles of beaches, with unprecedented destruction of marine and bird life.

Das Wrack des Riesentankers *Amoco Cadiz* vor der bretonischen Küste, Nordfrankreich, 26. März 1978. Mehr als 230.000 Tonnen Rohöl verpesteten Küste und Strände auf einer Länge von über 160 Kilometern, ein bis dato unbekanntes Ausmaß der Zerstörung vom Lebensraum der Fische und Vögel.

Epave du pétrolier géant l'*Amoco Cadiz* au large des côtes de la Bretagne, 26 mars 1978. 230 000 tonnes de mazout polluèrent plus de 160 kilomètres de plages, provoquant un anéantissement sans précédent de la vie marine et des oiseaux.

5. Cinema
Kino
Le cinéma

Francis Ford Coppola (front, reading *Variety*) and Robert de Niro (left) during a break in the filming of *The Godfather Part II*, 1974. Coppola said he enjoyed making this sequel more than the original: 'I've not been threatened with the sack every three weeks.'

Francis Ford Coppola (vorn im Bild, die *Variety* lesend) und Robert de Niro (links) während einer Pause bei den Dreharbeiten zu *Der Pate II*, 1974. Coppola kommentierte den Film mit den Worten, er möge den zweiten Teil lieber als den ersten, denn „man hat nicht alle drei Wochen damit gedroht, mich an die Luft zu setzen".

Francis Ford Coppola (au premier plan, lisant *Variety*) et Robert de Niro (à gauche) lors d'une pause pendant le tournage du *Parrain II*, 1974. Coppola raconta qu'il eut plus de plaisir à tourner cette suite que l'original : « Je n'ai pas été menacé toutes les trois semaines d'être foutu à la porte ».

5. Cinema
Kino
Le cinéma

The issues of the Seventies provided fertile ground both for Hollywood and Europe. A whole series of films reflected the preoccupations of the world. The war in Vietnam was the subject of many films, notably *The Deerhunter* and *Apocalypse Now*. *The China Syndrome* was released almost on the day that news broke of the disaster at Three Mile Island nuclear reactor.

But Hollywood was changing. Tinseltown was invaded by a new wave of directors, nicknamed The Movie Brats. Foremost among them were Francis Ford Coppola, Brian de Palma, George Lucas, Steven Spielberg and Martin Scorsese. Between them they directed a fistful of films that made enormous sums of money at the box office and were critical successes.

It seemed that nothing was sacred. The glitterati at Oscar ceremonies were shocked when George C Scott refused his award for *Patton* in 1970. Worse was to come when Marlon Brando turned down an Oscar for his role in *The Godfather* in 1973. Brando sent a native North American, Sasheen Littlefeather, to the ceremony with a message condemning the film industry 'for degrading the Indian and making a mockery of his character...'.

For a moment the razzmatazz was put on ice.

Die Ereignisse der siebziger Jahre lieferten sowohl der amerikanischen wie der europäischen Filmindustrie genügend Stoff. Eine ganze Serie von Filmen behandelte die aktuellen Geschehnisse. So war der Vietnamkrieg Thema zahlreicher Filme, vor allen anderen *Die durch die Hölle gehen* und *Apocalypse Now*. *Das China-Syndrom* kam fast auf den Tag genau in die Kinos, als sich der Reaktorunfall auf Three Mile Island ereignete.

Doch Hollywood machte einen Wandel durch. Die Stadt des falschen Glanzes wurde von einer Reihe junger Regisseure erobert, die schnell den Spitznamen Filmflegel erhielten. In erster Linie waren dies Francis Ford Coppola, Brian de Palma, George Lucas, Steven Spielberg und Martin Scorsese. Sie drehten eine Handvoll Filme, die enorme Summen einspielten und zugleich von der Kritik begeistert gefeiert wurden.

Scheinbar war nichts mehr heilig. Der Wirbel um die Oscar-Verleihung erlitt einen schweren Dämpfer, als George C. Scott 1970 die Auszeichnung für seine schauspielerische Leistung in *Patton – Panzer nach vorn* ablehnte. Doch es sollte noch schlimmer kommen, als Marlon Brando 1973 den Oscar für seine Rolle in *Der Pate* nicht entgegennehmen wollte und stattdessen die nordamerikanische Indianerin Sasheen Littlefeather zur Preisverleihung schickte. Dieser überbrachte eine Nachricht, in der Brando die Filmindustrie verurteilte, „weil sie den Indianer degradiert und aus seiner Rolle eine Farce macht …".

Für einen kurzen Moment stand der Rummel Hollywoods still.

Les événements des années soixante-dix constituèrent un matériau fertile aussi bien pour Hollywood que pour le cinéma européen. Toute une série de films refléta les préoccupations mondiales. La guerre du Viêt-nam fut le sujet de bien des films, notamment du *Voyage au bout de l'Enfer* et de *Apocalypse Now*. *Le Syndrome Chinois* sortit en salle presque le jour même où l'on apprit la catastrophe du réacteur nucléaire de Three Mile Island.

Pourtant Hollywood bougeait. La ville clinquante fut envahie par une nouvelle vague de réalisateurs que l'on surnommait les jeunes loups du cinéma. A leur tête se trouvaient Francis Ford Coppola, Brian de Palma, Georges Lucas, Steven Spielberg et Martin Scorsese. Ils réalisèrent une poignée de films qui rapportèrent énormément d'argent et furent loués par les critiques.

Il n'y avait plus rien de sacré. En 1970, George C. Scott choqua les rupins de la cérémonie des oscars en refusant son oscar pour *Patton*. Ce fut pire encore quand Marlon Brando refusa son oscar pour son rôle dans *Le Parrain* en 1973. Brando délégua à la cérémonie une Indienne nord-américaine, Sasheen Littlefeather, porteuse d'un message condamnant l'industrie du film pour avoir « avili les Indiens et les avoir tournés en dérision … ».

Le tape-à-l'œil fut mis au placard pendant quelque temps.

Orson Welles, December 1971. The early Seventies were the last good years in Welles's cinematic career. He played a high ranking officer in *Catch-22*, and received a special Oscar in 1971. Sadly, from then on it was all downhill.

Orson Welles, Dezember 1971. Die frühen siebziger Jahre zählen zu den letzten erfolgreichen Jahren seiner schauspielerischen Laufbahn. In *Catch-22* spielte er einen hochrangigen Offizier und erhielt dafür 1971 einen Sonder-Oscar. Leider ging es seitdem nur noch bergab.

Orson Welles, décembre 1971. Le début des années soixante-dix fut les dernières années fructueuses de sa carrière cinématographique. Il joua le rôle d'un officier supérieur dans *Catch-22* et reçut un oscar spécial en 1971. Malheureusement, tout périclita par la suite.

François Truffaut,
March 1978.
To Truffaut, Orson
Welles was the
master, the man
without whom the
modern cinema
would not have been
possible.

François Truffaut,
März 1978. Für
Truffaut war Orson
Welles der große
Meister, ohne den
das moderne Kino
nicht denkbar
gewesen wäre.

François Truffaut,
mars 1978. Il
considérait Orson
Welles comme un
maître sans qui le
cinéma moderne
n'aurait pas existé.

Clint Eastwood directing a scene from the film *Breezy*, December 1970. The film was coolly received, though acknowledged as 'technically attractive'. Eastwood had far more success in the Seventies in Westerns and as the maverick cop *Dirty Harry*.

Clint Eastwood bei der Regiearbeit an einer Szene aus dem Film *Begegnung am Vormittag*, Dezember 1970. Der Streifen wurde verhalten aufgenommen, wenngleich man ihn als „gut gemacht" einstufte. Mehr Erfolg hatte Eastwood in den siebziger Jahren als Westernheld und in seiner Rolle als einzelgängerischer Cop *Dirty Harry*.

Clint Eastwood, lors du tournage de *Breezy* , décembre 1970. Le film reçut un accueil peu favorable, bien que reconnu comme « techniquement séduisant ». Dans les années soixante-dix, Eastwood eut beaucoup plus de succès dans des westerns et dans le rôle de *Dirty Harry*, flic non-conformiste.

Italian 'Spaghetti
Western' film
director Sergio
Leone, brandishing
a pair of toy
revolvers but with
no spaghetti in sight,
1973.

Sergio Leone wurde
als Regisseur italieni-
scher „Spaghetti-
Western" berühmt.
Hier droht er mit
zwei Spielzeug-
revolvern, doch
Spaghetti sind
trotzdem nicht in
Sicht, 1973.

Sergio Leone,
réalisateur italien
de « westerns
spaghettis »,
brandissant une
paire de revolvers
pour enfants, mais
sans spaghettis en
vue, 1973.

Jack Nicholson, 1975 – the year in which he won an Oscar for his role in *One Flew Over the Cuckoo's Nest*. Nicholson's career blossomed in the Seventies, when he starred in such films as *Five Easy Pieces*, *The Last Detail* and *Chinatown*.

Jack Nicholson, 1975 – in dem Jahr als er den Oscar für seine Rolle in *Einer flog über das Kuckucksnest* gewann. Seine Karriere nahm in den siebziger Jahren einen Riesenaufschwung mit Filmen wie *Five Easy Pieces – Ein Mann sucht sich selbst*, *Das letzte Kommando* und *Chinatown*.

Jack Nicholson, 1975 – l'année où il reçut un oscar pour son rôle dans *Vol au-dessus d'un nid de coucou*. La carrière de Nicholson s'épanouit dans les années soixante-dix, dans des films dont il fut la vedette, tels *Cinq Pièces Faciles*, *La Dernière Corvée* et *Chinatown*.

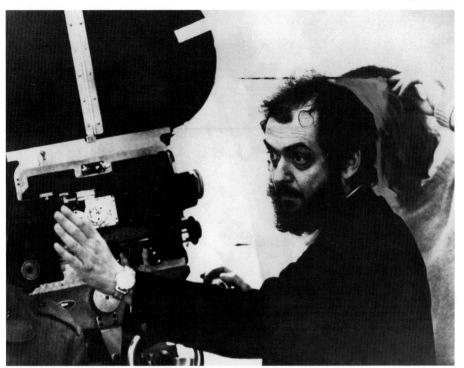

Director Stanley Kubrick on the set of *A Clockwork Orange*, December 1971. There were those who were sharpening their knives to attack the film for its violence even before Kubrick had finished making it.

Regisseur Stanley Kubrick bei den Dreharbeiten zu *Uhrwerk Orange*, Dezember 1971. Noch bevor der Film abgedreht war, erregte er wegen seiner Brutalität Aufsehen.

Le réalisateur Stanley Kubrick lors du tournage d'*Orange Mécanique*, décembre 1971. Certaines personnes commencèrent à affûter leurs couteaux pour attaquer le film à cause de sa violence bien avant la fin du tournage.

Woody Allen, October 1970. Allen was a prolific writer, director and actor in the Seventies, producing what many consider his best films: *Play It Again Sam*, *Love and Death*, *Annie Hall* and *Manhattan*.

Woody Allen, Oktober 1970. Der Drehbuchautor, Regisseur und Schauspieler drehte in den siebziger Jahren zahlreiche Filme, die viele für seine besten halten: *Mach's noch einmal Sam*, *Die letzte Nacht des Boris Gruschenko*, *Der Stadtneurotiker* und *Manhattan*.

Woody Allen, octobre 1970. Dans les années soixante-dix, Allen fut à la fois un auteur, réalisateur et acteur prolifique et produisit ce que beaucoup considèrent comme ses meilleurs films : *Tombe les Filles et Tais-Toi*, *Guerre et Amour*, *Annie Hall* et *Manhattan*.

Diane Keaton, 1975. Keaton was Allen's co-star in *Annie Hall*, a film that Allen described as a 'nervous romance'.

Diane Keaton, 1975. Sie war Woody Allens Filmpartnerin in *Der Stadtneurotiker*. Der Regisseur kommentierte den Film als eine „nervöse Romanze".

Diane Keaton, 1975. Keaton fut la vedette de *Annie Hall* aux côtés de Woody Allen qu'il décrit comme une « romance névrotique ».

Roman Polanski (right) talks to Hugh Hefner and Francesca Annis
(centre), February 1971. Hefner and his Playboy empire were backing
Polanski's 'brutalized' version of *Macbeth*, which starred Annis.

Roman Polanski (rechts) im Gespräch mit Hugh Hefner und Francesca
Annis (Mitte), Februar 1971. Hefner und sein Playboy-Imperium
stärkten Polanskis „brutalisierter" Version des *Macbeth* den Rücken, in
welcher Annis die Hauptrolle spielte.

Roman Polanski (à droite) converse avec Hugh Hefner et Francesca
Annis (au centre), février 1971. Hefner et l'empire financier de
Playboy aidèrent Polanski à réaliser sa version « brutalisée » de
Macbeth, avec Annis dans le rôle principal.

Isabella Rossellini and Martin Scorsese, shortly
before their marriage, 1979. Rossellini is the
daughter of the Italian film director Roberto
Rossellini and Ingrid Bergman.

Isabella Rossellini und Martin Scorsese kurz vor
ihrer Hochzeit, 1979. Rossellini ist die Tochter des
italienischen Filmregisseurs Roberto Rossellini und
der Schauspielerin Ingrid Bergman.

Isabella Rossellini et Martin Scorsese, peu avant leur
mariage, 1979. Rossellini est la fille du réalisateur
italien Roberto Rossellini et d'Ingrid Bergman.

August 1973. Robert Redford, framed by the arches of Waterloo
Bridge, outside the National Film Theatre on London's South Bank. It
was a busy time for Redford. In 18 months he made *The Candidate*,
The Way We Were and *The Sting*.

August 1973. Robert Redford, eingerahmt von den Bogen der
Waterloo Bridge vor dem National Film Theatre auf Londons
Südseite. Es war eine produktive Zeit für Redford. In 18 Monaten
drehte er *Der Kandidat*, *So wie wir waren* und *Der Clou*.

Août 1973. Robert Redford, photographié sous les arches du pont
Waterloo, devant le National Film Theatre sur la rive sud de Londres.
Redford était très demandé. En 18 mois, il tourna *Votez McKay*, *Nos
plus belles Années* et *L'Arnaque*.

Dustin Hoffman as Carl Bernstein on the set of *All The President's Men*, July 1975. The film also starred Redford, and was a dramatization of the part played by the *Washington Post* reporters in uncovering the Watergate Affair.

Dustin Hoffman als Carl Bernstein beim Dreh von *Die Unbestechlichen*, Juli 1975. Hoffman und Redford spielten die beiden *Washington-Post*-Reporter, die den Watergate-Skandal aufdeckten.

Dustin Hoffman dans le rôle de Carl Bernstein lors du tournage *Les Hommes du président*, juillet 1975. Ce film adapta à l'écran le rôle joué par les reporters du *Washington Post* dans l'affaire du Watergate. Redford y tenait aussi un rôle principal.

May 1977. Arnold Schwarzenegger, then
famous as 'Mr Universe', bulges his muscles
for members of the Folies-Bergère on the
beach at the Cannes Film Festival.

Mai 1977. Arnold Schwarzenegger, damals
noch der berühmte „Mr. Universum", läßt
während der Filmfestspiele von Cannes am
Strand seine Muskeln für die Damen der
Folies-Bergère spielen.

Mai 1977. Arnold Schwarzenegger, connu à
l'époque comme « Monsieur Univers », genfle
ses muscles pour les filles des Folies-Bergère,
sur la plage du Festival de Cannes.

Tim Curry, in a drag
outfit from *The
Rocky Horror
Picture Show*, poses
for the camera,
1975.

Tim Curry, Travestit
in der *Rocky Horror
Picture Show*, posiert
hier vor der Kamera,
1975.

Tim Curry, dans un
accoutrement de
travesti du *Rocky
Horror Picture
Show*, pose devant la
caméra, 1975.

Olivia Newton-John and John Travolta at the premier of *Grease*,
Chicago, 1978. They were mobbed by fans. The film, a nostalgic
recreation of a 1950s high school, was an enormous success.

Olivia Newton-John und John Travolta bei der Premiere von *Grease* in
Chicago, 1978. Sie waren von Fans umringt. Der Film war eine
nostalgische Wiederbelebung vom Highschool Leben der fünfziger
Jahre und wurde ein Riesenerfolg.

Olivia Newton-John et John Travolta lors de la première de *Grease*,
Chicago, 1978. Ils furent pris d'assaut par leurs fans. Ce film, un
divertissement nostalgique sur les collèges des années cinquante, eut
un énorme succès.

Burt Reynolds and Liza Minnelli set out to hit the town, December 1975. At the time, they were both at the height of their careers.

Burt Reynolds und Liza Minelli machen sich auf den Weg, um die Stadt zu erobern, Dezember 1975. Beide standen damals auf dem Höhepunkt ihrer Karriere.

Burt Reynolds et Liza Minnelli débarquent en ville, décembre 1975. A cette époque, ils étaient tous deux au sommet de leur carrière.

Donald Sutherland and Shirley MacLaine, 1976. Sutherland's big successes in the early Seventies had been *M*A*S*H* and *Klute*. After four years away from films, MacLaine returned to Hollywood to make *The Turning Point* in 1977.

Donald Sutherland und Shirley MacLaine, 1976. Sutherlands größte Erfolge Anfang der siebziger Jahre waren *M*A*S*H* und *Klute*. Shirley MacLaine hatte vier Jahre pausiert und kehrte nun nach Hollywood zurück, um 1977 *Am Wendepunkt* zu drehen.

Donald Sutherland et Shirley MacLaine, 1976. Les grands succès de Sutherland au début années soixante-dix furent *M. A. S. H.* et *Klute*. Après avoir arrêté de tourner pendant quatre ans, Shirley MacLaine revint à Hollywood pour faire *Cran d'Arrêt* en 1977.

Ryan O'Neal and
Barbra Streisand on
the set of *What's Up
Doc?*, March 1972.
Streisand was
proud to 'arrive' in
Hollywood without
changing her teeth,
her nose, or
her name.

Ryan O'Neal und
Barbra Streisand bei
den Dreharbeiten zu
Is' was, Doc?, März
1972. Barbra Strei-
sand war stolz da-
rauf, in Hollywood
„anzukommen",
ohne ihre Zähne,
ihre Nase oder ihren
Namen verändert
zu haben.

Ryan O'Neal et
Barbra Streisand lors
du tournage de *On
s'fait la valise,
Docteur ?*, mars
1972. Streisand était
fière d'avoir réussi à
Hollywood sans
opération de chi-
rurgie esthétique et
sans avoir changé
de nom.

Al Pacino, the young 'Don', takes a stroll along Madison Avenue, New York City, 1976.

Al Pacino, der junge „Don" bummelt über die Madison Avenue in New York, 1976.

Al Pacino, le jeune « Don », flâne le long de Madison Avenue, New York, 1976.

Gene Hackman as
'Popeye Doyle'
during the filming of
*French Connection
II* on location in
Marseille,
September 1974.

Gene Hackman als
„Glotzauge Doyle"
während der Auf-
nahmen am Drehort
Marseille zu *French
Connection II*,
September 1974.

Gene Hackman dans
le rôle de « Popeye
Doyle » durant le
tournage de *French
Connection II*,
Marseille, septembre
1974.

July 1975. Robert de Niro poses in front of his
shiny Mercedes. It was the year in which he won an
Oscar as Best Supporting Actor for his part in *The
Godfather Part II*.

Juli 1975. Robert de Niro posiert vor seinem blank-
polierten Mercedes. In dem Jahr gewann er einen
Oscar als bester Nebendarsteller in *Der Pate II*.

Juillet 1975. Robert de Niro pose devant sa
Mercedes étincelante. Il reçut cette année-là l'oscar
du deuxième rôle masculin pour *Le Parrain II*.

Sylvester Stallone directs a scene from *Paradise Alley*, May 1978. As a change from boxing in *Rocky*, Stallone played the part of a wrestler. 'People don't credit me with much of a brain,' he said, 'so why should I disillusion them?'

Sylvester Stallone als Regisseur bei einer Szene für *Vorhof zum Paradies*, Mai 1978. Als Abwechslung zu seinen Rollen als Boxer in *Rocky*, spielte er nun einen Ringkämpfer. „Die Leute trauen mir nicht zu, daß ich viel im Kopf habe," meinte er, „also warum sollte ich ihnen ihren Glauben nehmen?"

Sylvester Stallone met en scène *La Taverne de l'Enfer*, mai 1978. Pour changer de son rôle de boxeur dans *Rocky*, il y joua le personnage d'un lutteur. « Les gens pensent que je n'ai pas beaucoup de cervelle, « déclara-t-il, » alors, pourquoi les décevoir ? »

Brigitte Bardot (back to camera) goes for a row with a friend and five dogs, 1975. Bardot had retired from the screen two years earlier, and had already begun her work for the welfare of animals.

Brigitte Bardot (mit dem Rücken zur Kamera) unternimmt mit einer Freundin und fünf Hunden eine Rudertour, 1975. Bardot hatte sich vor zwei Jahren aus dem Filmgeschäft zurückgezogen und widmete sich nun dem Tierschutz.

Brigitte Bardot (dos à la caméra) fait du bateau en compagnie d'un ami et de cinq chiens, 1975. Bardot s'était retirée de la scène deux ans plus tôt et avait commencé à militer activement pour la protection des animaux.

Meryl Streep, December 1979. Taking time out from the
movies, she is seen here in preparation for Shakespeare in
the Park's production of *Taming of the Shrew*, Central Park,
New York.

Meryl Streep, Dezember 1979. Während eines Auszeit vom
Film, ist sie hier bei den Vorbereitungen zu Parks Shakespeare-
Produktion der *Widerspenstigen Zähmung* zu sehen, Central
Park, New York.

Meryl Streep, décembre 1979. Quittant un peu les caméras,
on l'apperçoit dans la préparation de *La mégère apprivoisée* de
Shakespeare, une production de Park, Central Park, New York.

Roman Polanski and Nastassja Kinski, May 1979. He was announcing his return to the United States, after he had been charged with having an illicit relationship with an under-age girl.

Roman Polanski und Nastassja Kinski, Mai 1979. Er gibt seine Rückkehr in die USA bekannt, nachdem er be- schuldigt worden war, eine gesetzes- widrige Affäre mit einer Minderjähri- gen zu haben.

Roman Polanski et Nastassja Kinski, mai 1979. Il annonce son retour aux Etats-Unis après avoir été accusé de relations illicites avec une mineure.

June 1976. Jane
Fonda auctions a
book by Cesar
Estrada Chavez at a
New York charity
party. Chavez had
promoted a nation-
wide boycott of
Californian grapes
in 1970.

Juni 1976. Jane
Fonda versteigert ein
Buch von Cesar
Estrada Chavez auf
einer New Yorker
Wohltätigkeitsveran-
staltung. Chavez
hatte zu einem
landesweiten Boy-
kott kalifornischer
Weintrauben aufge-
rufen, 1970.

Juin 1976. Jane
Fonda met aux
enchères un livre
de Cesar Estrada
Chavez lors d'une
vente de bien-
faisance à New York.
Chavez avait en-
couragé le boycott
national des raisins
de Californie
en 1970.

6. The Arts
Die Kunst
Les arts

June 1975. David Hockney on the set he designed for a Glyndebourne Opera production of Stravinsky's *The Rake's Progress*. Hockney had produced a set of etchings based on the same theme in the Sixties.

Juni 1975. David Hockney vor dem Bühnenbild, das er für die Strawinsky-Oper *Der Wüstling* entworfen hatte, die beim Opern-festival von Glyndebourne aufgeführt wurde. Hockney hatte bereits in den sechziger Jahren eine Serie von Radierungen zum selben Thema geschaffen.

Juin 1975. David Hockney devant les décors qu'il dessina pour *The Rake's Progress* de Stravinski produit par l'Opéra de Glyndebourne. Hockney réalisa dans les années soixante un ensemble de gravures basées sur le même thème.

6. The Arts
Die Kunst
Les arts

Modern giants from every medium of the arts departed in the Seventies: Stravinsky, E M Forster, Picasso, Duke Ellington, Shostakovich, Barbara Hepworth and the divine Maria Callas. The old order was further damaged when a deranged Hungarian named Laszlo Toth took a hammer to Michaelangelo's *Pietà* in St Peter's, Rome, in May 1972.

But there were always new talents to celebrate. In the world of music there was the minimalist *Drumming* of Steve Reich, and the first of Philip Glass's four operas, *Einstein on the Beach*. In 1970 Pierre Boulez became director of the influential Institut de Recherche et de Coordination Acoustique/Musique. Hans Werner Henze devoted most of his time to such works for Music Theatre as *El Cimarron* and *We Come to the River*.

In painting Pop Art still flourished, though Andy Warhol spent more time on portrait-painting and film-making, and Peter Blake gave it all up to found the Brotherhood of Ruralists in 1975. Georg Baselitz and Francesco Clemente were the leaders of the school of Neo-Expressionism, and feminists demanded a reassessment of the entire history of art.

At the grass-roots level, there was a proliferation of festivals of music, drama, opera, dance, poetry and literature, all over the world.

Einige der unumstrittenen Größten der modernen Künste verstarben in den siebziger Jahren: Strawinsky, E. M. Forster, Picasso, Duke Ellington, Schostakowitsch, Barbara Hepworth und die göttliche Maria Callas. Als im Mai 1972 der geistig verwirrte Ungar Laszlo Toth mit einem Hammer auf die *Pietà* Michelangelos in der Peterskirche von Rom einschlägt, ist das nur ein weiterer Schlag gegen die alte Ordnung der Dinge.

Stattdessen gab es immer neue Talente zu feiern. Steve Reich begeisterte die Musikfans mit seinem minimalistischen *Drumming*, und Philip Glass führte die erste seiner vier Opern, *Einstein on the Beach*, auf. Pierre Boulez wurde 1970 Direktor des einflußreichen Institut de

Recherche et de Coordination Acoustique/Musique. Hans Werner Henze widmete den größten Teil seiner Zeit Werken des Musiktheaters wie *El Cimarron* und *Wir erreichen den Fluß*.

Eine der Hauptfiguren der Pop-art, Andy Warhol, beschäftigte sich nun vermehrt mit der Porträtmalerei und dem Filmemachen, wohingegen Peter Blake die Pop-art ganz aufgab und 1975 die Bruderschaft der Ruralisten gründete. Georg Baselitz und Francesco Clemente waren die führenden Persönlichkeiten der neoexpressionistischen Schule, die Feministen forderten eine Neuschreibung der gesamten Kunstgeschichte.

Auf der ganzen Welt war der Boden bereitet für Musikfestivals, Theater- und Opernaufführungen, Tanz, Dichtung und Literatur.

Des géants modernes de tous les milieux des arts moururent dans les années soixante-dix : Stravinski, E. M. Forster, Picasso, Duke Ellington, Chostakovitch, Barbara Hepworth et la divine Maria Callas. L'ancien état des choses fut encore plus endommagé lorsqu'un Hongrois à l'esprit dérangé, nommé Laszlo Toth, s'attaqua au marteau à la *Pietà* de Michel-Ange dans la cathédrale Saint-Pierre de Rome, en mai 1972.

Mais il restait d'abondantes de nouvelles œuvres à fêter : en musique, le *Drumming* minimaliste de Steve Reich, ainsi que le premier des quatre opéras de Philip Glass, *Einstein on the Beach*. En 1970, Pierre Boulez devint directeur de l'important Institut de Recherche et de Coordination Acoustique/Musique. Hans Werner Henze consacra la plupart de son temps à créer des œuvres musicales pour le théâtre, telles que *El Cimarron* et *We Come to the River*.

En peinture, le Pop art continuait à prospérer, bien qu'Andy Warhol passât plus de temps à peindre des portraits et à faire des films et que Peter Blake abandonnât tout pour fonder la Confrérie des ruralistes en 1975. Georg Baselitz et Francesco Clemente étaient les leaders de l'école néo-expressioniste et les féministes demandèrent un réexamen de toute l'histoire de l'art.

Plus au ras des pâquerettes, il y eut dans le monde entier une prolifération de festivals de musique, de théâtre, d'opéra, de danse, de poésie et de littérature.

Bridget Riley in front of one of her Op Art masterpieces, 1979. Riley painted large canvases of overall flat patterns, often in black and white, with undulating lines which dazzled the beholder, creating an illusion of movement.

Die Op-Art-Künstlerin Bridget Riley vor einem ihrer Meisterwerke, 1979. Sie bemalte riesige Leinwände mit gleichmäßigen Flächenmustern, oftmals schwarzweiß. Das Auge des Betrachters wird durch wellenförmige Linien verwirrt, die die Illusion von Bewegung schaffen.

Bridget Riley devant l'un de ses chefs-d'œuvres Op art, 1979. Riley réalisa d'immenses toiles aux motifs plats d'un bout à l'autre, souvent en noir et blanc, aux lignes ondulées qui aveuglaient les spectateurs, créant une illusion de mouvement.

Allen Jones, English
painter, sculptor
and printmaker,
with his Pop Art
coffee table, 1972.

Allen Jones, engli-
scher Maler, Bild-
hauer und Grafiker,
und sein Couchtisch
im Stil der
Pop-art, 1972.

Allen Jones, peintre,
sculpteur et graveur
anglais, avec sa table
de café Pop art,
1972.

New York, April 1977. Andy Warhol with one of his portraits from the Seventies, *Princess of Iran*. Warhol's portraits were usually executed in series, as in this case. In 1973 he produced 10 portraits of Chairman Mao.

New York, April 1977. Andy Warhol vor seinen Porträts der *Princess of Iran*, die in den siebziger Jahren entstanden. Es gehörte zu Warhols Markenzeichen, häufig eine ganze Porträt-Serie zu malen. Im Jahre 1973 hatte er 10 Bildnisse von Chinas Staatschef Mao gemalt.

New York, avril 1977. Andy Warhol avec l'un de ses portraits des années soixante-dix, *La Princesse d'Iran*. Les portraits de Warhol furent généralement exécutés en série, comme dans ce cas. En 1973, il réalisa 10 portraits du président Mao.

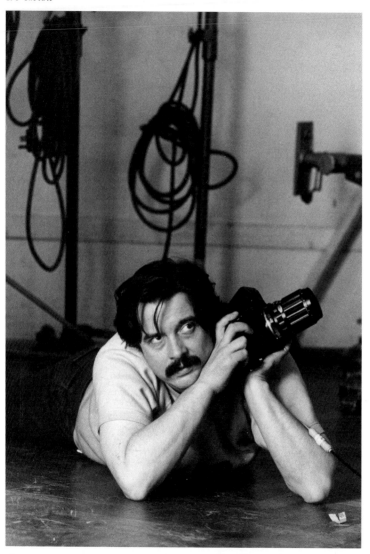

David Bailey at work on the last *Vogue* photographic session from the Hanover Square studios, London, June 1975.

David Bailey bei seiner letzten Fotoproduktion für die *Vogue* in den Hanover Square Studios in London, Juni 1975.

David Bailey lors de la dernière séance de photos pour *Vogue* aux studios Hanover Square, Londres, juin 1975.

1970. The British painter Francis Bacon finds London street scaffolding either a support or an obstacle.

1970. Für den englischen Maler Francis Bacon stellt dieses Baugerüst in einer Londoner Straße entweder eine Stütze oder ein Hindernis dar.

1970. Le peintre anglais Francis Bacon hésite : les échafaudages de cette rue de Londres sont-ils un appui ou un obstacle ?

Christo Javacheff, the Bulgarian born avant-garde artist, struggles to wrap the cove at King's Beach, Newport, Massachusetts, October 1974. The woven polypropylene drape measured 14,800 square yards (12,600 square metres) and weighed eight tons.

Der gebürtige Bulgare Christo Jawatcheff versucht, die kleine Bucht am King's Beach in Newport, zu verhüllen, Massachusetts, Oktober 1974. Die Drapierung aus gewebten Polypropylen war 12.600 Quadratmeter lang und wog 8 Tonnen.

Christo Javacheff, l'artiste avant-gardiste d'origine bulgare se débat pour envelopper la baie de King's Beach, Newport, Massachusetts, octobre 1974. L'étoffe tissée en polypropylène mesurait 12 600 mètres carrés et pesait huit tonnes.

American sculptor Claes Oldenburg, March 1975. Oldenburg specialized in large forms of small objects.

Der amerikanische Bildhauer Claes Oldenburg, März 1975. Der Künstler hatte sich auf die Vergrößerung kleiner Objekte spezialisiert.

Le sculpteur américain Claes Oldenburg, mars 1975. Oldenburg se spécialisa dans la représentation agrandie de petits objets.

November 1976.
Sveva Vigeveno's
portrait of the Czech
novelist Milan
Kundera, author of
*The Unbearable
Lightness of Being.*

November 1976.
Sveva Vigevenos
Porträt des tschechi-
schen Schriftstellers
Milan Kundera,
Autor von *Die
unerträgliche
Leichtigkeit des
Seins.*

Novembre 1976.
Portrait de l'écrivain
tchèque Milan
Kundera, auteur de
*L'Insoutenable
Légèreté de l'être*,
par le photographe
Sveva Vigeveno.

Alexander Solzhenitsyn approaches the Norwegian coastline, 27 February 1974.
Two weeks earlier he had been exiled from the Soviet Union without warning,
following the publication of *The Gulag Archipelago*.

Alexander Solschenizyn auf dem Weg nach Norwegen, 27. Februar 1974. Zwei
Wochen zuvor war er ohne Vorankündigung aus der Sowjetunion ausgebürgert
worden, nachdem sein Buch *Archipel Gulag* erschienen war.

Alexandre Soljenitsyne approche des côtes norvégiennes, 27 février 1974. Deux
semaines plus tôt, l'Union soviétique l'avait expulsé sans avertissement, après la
publication de *L'Archipel du Goulag*.

Norman Mailer,
American writer,
October 1970.
A regular protester
in the Sixties,
Mailer mellowed in
the Seventies.

Norman Mailer,
amerikanischer
Schriftsteller,
Oktober 1970. Als
ständiger Kritiker
in den sechziger
Jahren, wurde er in
den siebziger Jahren
regelrecht zahm.

Norman Mailer,
écrivain américain,
octobre 1970. Con-
testataire infatigable
dans les années
soixante, il mit de
l'eau dans son vin
dans la décennie
suivante.

Erich Auerbach's photo of the violinist Isaac Stern, Claridges Hotel, London, November 1970. Stern is examining other portraits of him by Auerbach.

Erich Auerbach nahm dieses Foto des Geigers Isaac Stern im Claridges Hotel in London auf, November 1970. Stern betrachtet kritisch andere Porträts, die Auerbach von ihm gemacht hat.

Le violoniste Isaac Stern, photographié par Erich Auerbach à l'hôtel Claridges, Londres, novembre 1970. Stern examine l'un de ses portraits réalisés par Auerbach.

Tony McGrath's portrait of the French conductor, composer and musical director Pierre Boulez, 1971. At the time, Boulez was musical adviser and conductor of the Cleveland Orchestra, and music director of the New York Philharmonic.

Tony McGrath's Fotografie des französischen Dirigenten, Komponisten und Musikdirektors Pierre Boulez, 1971. Zu jener Zeit war Boulez der musikalische Leiter und Dirigent des Cleveland Orchestra und Musikdirektor an der New Yorker Philharmonie.

Portrait de Pierre Boulez, compositeur et chef d'orchestre français, par Tony McGrath, 1971. A cette époque, Boulez était conseiller musical, chef de l'Orchestre de Cleveland et directeur musical du Philharmonique de New York.

London, February 1970. Leonard Bernstein, American conductor, composer and pianist, in full flow as he rehearses the London Symphony Orchestra at St Pancras Town Hall.

London, Februar 1970. Leonard Bernstein, amerikanischer Dirigent, Komponist und Pianist, ist bei den Proben mit dem Londoner Sinfonieorchester in der St. Pancras Town Hall voll in seinem Element.

Londres, février 1970. Léonard Bernstein, chef d'orchestre américain, compositeur et pianiste, en pleine action, lors d'une répétition avec l'Orchestre symphonique de Londres au St. Pancras Town Hall.

The Russian dancer
Mikhail
Baryshnikov,
October 1975.
Baryshnikov
dramatically raced
to political asylum
in Toronto in 1974.

Der russische
Tänzer Michail
Baryschnikow,
Oktober 1975.
Baryschnikow bat
unter dramatischen
Umständen 1974 in
Toronto um Asyl.

Le danseur russe
Mikhail
Baryshnikow,
octobre 1975.
Baryshnikow lutta
farouchement
pour obtenir l'asile
politique à Toronto
en 1974.

Rudolf Nureyev
on the beach in
Monaco with fellow
dancer Antoinette
Sibley, August 1973.
He had already
spent 12 years in the
West.

Rudolf Nurejew
mit Tanzpartnerin
Antoinette Sibley am
Strand von Monaco,
August 1973. Er
lebte bereits seit 12
Jahren im Westen.

Rudolf Noureïev, sur
la plage de Monaco
en compagnie de sa
collègue Antoinette
Sibley, août 1973.
Il était déjà passé
depuis 12 ans à
l'Ouest.

7. Pop
Popmusik
La musique pop

London, February 1976. Marc Bolan on stage at the Lyceum Ballroom, The Strand. Bolan was a founder member of T-Rex, whose early Seventies hits included 'Hot Love' and 'Get It On'. He was killed in a car crash in September 1977.

London, Februar 1976. Marc Bolan auf der Bühne im Lyceum Ballroom, The Strand. Bolan gehörte zu den Gründungsmitgliedern der T-Rex, die Anfang der siebziger Jahre mit Hits wie „Hot Love" und „Get It On" bekannt wurden. Er starb im September 1977 bei einem Autounfall.

Londres, février 1976. Marc Bolan sur la scène du Lyceum Ballroom, The Strand. Bolan fut l'un des membres fondateurs du groupe T-Rex, dont les succès au début des années soixante-dix étaient « Hot Love » et « Get It On ». Il mourut dans un accident de voiture en septembre 1977.

7. Pop
Popmusik
La musique pop

The Seventies began tragically with the deaths in rapid succession of Jimi Hendrix, Janis Joplin, and Jim Morrison of The Doors. The Beatles split up. The Bee Gees got it together again. The Stones went rolling on. Abba sold more records than any other band. Led Zeppelin were the biggest – if not the heaviest – of the Heavy Metal bands.

It was the decade of the supergroup: Crosby, Stills and Nash; The Who; Cream; Emerson, Lake and Palmer. Tens of thousands flocked to live performances by these bands, but there were those critics who claimed technical perfection and beautifully crafted albums didn't always produce inspiring music.

Glam-rock made an entrance, with Marc Bolan and David Bowie appearing in psychedelic costumes that drove fans to frenzy. Lovely to look at, but light to listen to.

Punk was big in Europe and gained a painted toehold in New York, Detroit and a few other US cities. The Sex Pistols roared to fame with angry versions of anything from 'My Way' to 'God Save The Queen'. 'Actually,' said one of The Pistols, 'we're not into music. We're into chaos.'

Elvis Presley bowed out on 16 August 1977. Within a week he was back at the top of the American charts.

Die siebziger Jahre begannen tragisch. Kurz hintereinander starben Jimi Hendrix, Janis Joplin und Jim Morrison von den Doors. Die Beatles trennten sich. Die Bee Gees rauften sich wieder zusammen. Die Stones „rollten" weiter. Abba verkaufte mehr Platten als jede andere Popgruppe. Led Zeppelin war die bekannteste – wenn nicht die wildeste – der Heavy-Metal-Bands.

Das Jahrzehnt der Supergruppen war angebrochen: Crosby, Stills and Nash; The Who; Cream; Emerson, Lake and Palmer. Zehntausende von Fans strömten zu ihren Live-

Konzerten, aber es gab auch kritische Stimmen die behaupteten, daß technische Perfektion und wunderbar gestaltete Plattencover nicht unbedingt auch inspirierte Musik bedeuteten.

Glamour-Rock war plötzlich angesagt. Marc Bolan und David Bowie brachten ihre Fans mit psychedelischem Bühnenoutfit zur Raserei. Hübsch anzusehen, aber anspruchslos.

Die Punks feierten in Europa große Erfolge und konnten auch nach New York, Detroit und in einige andere amerikanische Metropolen ihren bunten Touch bringen. Die Sex Pistols brüllten sich zu Ruhm mit aggressiven Variationen über alles mögliche, was schon einmal da gewesen war, von „My Way" bis hin zu „God Save the Queen". „Eigentlich sind wir keine Musiker, im Grunde sind wir Chaoten", so das Statement eines Bandmitglieds.

Elvis Presley starb am 16. August 1977. Innerhalb einer Woche waren seine Songs zurück an der Spitze der amerikanischen Hitlisten.

Les années soixante-dix débutèrent de façon tragique avec la succession rapide des décès de Jimi Hendrix, Janis Joplin et de Jim Morrison des Doors. Les Beatles se séparèrent. Les Bee Gees reformèrent un groupe. Les Rolling Stones continuèrent à rouler leur bosse. Abba vendit plus de disques que n'importe quel autre groupe. Led Zeppelin était le plus grand – si ce n'est le plus « heavy » – des groupes Heavy Metal.

Ce fut la décennie des supergroupes : Crosby, Stills and Nash ; les Who ; Cream ; Emerson, Lake and Palmer. Des dizaines de milliers de fans affluèrent aux concerts live de ces groupes, mais des critiques affirmèrent que perfection technique et maquettes élaborées des couvertures de disques ne suffisaient pas toujours à faire de la bonne musique.

Ce fut le début du glam-rock, avec Marc Bolan et David Bowie dans des costumes psychédéliques qui provoquèrent la frénésie des fans. Joli à regarder, mais facile à écouter.

Les punks avaient un succès fou en Europe et apportèrent une touche colorée à New York, Détroit et quelques autres villes américaines. Les hurlements rageurs des Sex Pistols leur apportèrent la célébrité, de « My Way » jusqu'à « God Save The Queen ». « En fait, » déclara l'un des Pistols, « nous ne faisons pas de la musique, nous faisons du désordre. »

Elvis Presley tira sa révérence le 16 août 1977. En moins d'une semaine, il était de retour en tête du hit-parade américain.

Mick Jagger in concert, 1976. The Stones were still grabbing the headlines in the Seventies. Jagger was shot in the hand while filming *Ned Kelly*, there was the usual drug trouble, and the Reverend Jesse Jackson found their 'Some Girls' album racist.

Mick Jagger in Aktion, 1976. Die Stones machten in den siebziger Jahren immer noch Schlagzeilen. Während der Dreharbeiten zu *Ned Kelly* wurde Jagger durch einen Schuß in die Hand verletzt. Es gab die üblichen Drogengeschichten, und der Geistliche Jesse Jackson verurteilte ihr Album „Some Girls" als rassistisch.

Mick Jagger en concert, 1976. Au cours des années soixante-dix, les Stones accaparaient encore la une des journaux. Jagger fut blessé d'une balle à la main alors qu'il tournait *Ned Kelly*, il y eut les inévitables problèmes de drogues et le révérend Jesse Jackson décréta que leur album « Some Girls » était raciste.

David Bowie at the Hammersmith Odeon, London, July 1973. After the concert he announced, 'All my forthcoming American dates have been cancelled.' Less than 10 months later, the US tour was reinstated.

David Bowie bei einem Bühnenauftritt im Hammersmith Odeon, London, Juli 1973. Nach dem Konzert gab er bekannt: „Alle weiteren Auftritte in den USA sind gestrichen." 10 Monate später fand die Amerika-Tournee doch noch statt.

David Bowie au Hammersmith Odeon, Londres, juillet 1973. Après le concert, il annonça : « Tous mes prochains concerts aux Etats-Unis sont annulés ». Moins de 10 mois plus tard, la tournée américaine fut rétablie.

Peter Gould's revealing portrait of Elvis Aaron Presley in one of the King's last appearances before his death, 1977.

Peter Gould nahm dieses vielsagende Foto von Elvis Aaron Presley auf. Es war einer der letzten Auftritte vor seinem Tode, 1977.

Portrait révélateur d'Elvis Aaron Presley par Peter Gould, lors de l'une des dernières apparitions du King avant sa mort, 1977.

Rod Stewart on
stage at Olympia,
London, 1979.
'The name of the
game is to get
people there…'

Rod Stewart wäh-
rend eines Auf-
tritts im Olympia,
London, 1979. „Das
Spiel geht so, die
Leute dorthin zu
kriegen …"

Rod Stewart sur la
scène de l'Olympia,
Londres, 1979.
« Ce qui compte,
c'est d'attirer les
gens ici … »

January 1972.
Heart-throb and
pop singer Tom
Jones in a scene
from a television
programme about
London Bridge.

Januar 1972. Her-
zensbrecher und
Popsänger Tom
Jones in einer Fern-
sehsendung über die
London Bridge.

Janvier 1972. Tom
Jones, chanteur pop
et coqueluche de ces
dames, dans une
émission télévisée
sur le pont
de Londres.

Cliff Richard and
Olivia Newton-
John, February
1971. Olivia was
appearing as a guest
on Cliff's television
programme.

Cliff Richard und
Olivia Newton-
John, Februar 1971.
Olivia trat als
Stargast in Cliffs
Fernsehsendung auf.

Cliff Richard et
Olivia Newton-
John, février 1971.
Olivia était l'invitée
d'une émission
télévisée de Cliff.

1973. Elton John – pop singer, composer, pianist and chairman of Watford Football Club – leads his team onto the pitch.

1973. Elton John – Popsänger, Song-Schreiber, Pianist und Vorsitzender des Fußballclubs von Watford – führt seine Mannschaft aufs Spielfeld.

1973. Elton John – chanteur pop, compositeur, pianiste et président du club de football de Watford – mène son équipe sur le terrain.

The Swedish group Abba in concert, February 1979. (Left to right) Benny Andersson, Annifrid Lyngstad, Agnetha Fältskog and Björn Ulvaeus.

Die schwedische Band Abba bei einem Bühnenauftritt, Februar 1979. (Von links nach rechts) Benny Andersson, Annifrid Lyngstad, Agnetha Fältskog und Björn Ulvaeus.

Le groupe suédois Abba en concert, février 1979. (De gauche à droite) Benny Andersson, Annifrid Lyngstad, Agnetha Fältskog et Björn Ulvaeus.

The Osmonds play the Gröna Lund, Stockholm, July 1975.
Fifteen teenage girl fans fainted, but the show went on. For a
while, the world was in the grip of Osmondmania, but sanity
ultimately prevailed.

Die Osmonds spielen in Gröna Lunds, Stockholm, Juli 1975.
Fünfzehn Mädchen fielen in Ohnmacht, aber die Show ging
weiter. Eine Zeitlang schien die Welt vom Osmond-Fieber
befallen zu sein, doch schließlich gesundete sie wieder.

Les Osmonds jouent au Gröna Lund, Stockholm, juillet 1975.
Quinze adolescentes s'évanouirent, mais le spectacle continua.
Le monde fut envoûté pendant quelque temps par l'« osmondie »;
puis le bon sens prévalut.

October 1972. The Jackson Five, soul pop brothers
from Indiana, in the early days of their career. Michael
Jackson (far left) was still two years away from his first
big hit, 'Ben'.

Oktober 1972. Die Jackson Five, Soul-Pop-Brüder aus
Indiana standen damals am Anfang ihrer Karriere.
Michael Jackson (ganz links) konnte erst mit „Ben"
zwei Jahre später seinen ersten großen Hit landen.

Octobre 1972. Les frères Jackson Five de l'Indiana,
chanteurs soul et pop, au début de leur carrière.
Michael Jackson (tout à gauche) connaîtra deux ans
plus tard son premier grand succès, « Ben ».

A vast audience gathers at the White City,
London, for a concert by David Cassidy, 28
May 1974. Cassidy was regarded as a very
clean-cut performer. The only vice he
admitted to was biting his nails.

Eine riesige Fan-Gemeinde beim Konzert von
David Cassidy, White City, London, 28. Mai
1974. Cassidy galt als äußerst gepflegter
Künstler. Die einzige Unart, die er sich
erlaubte, war Fingernägelkauen.

Foule rassemblée à White City à Londres pour
le concert de David Cassidy, 28 mai 1974.
Cassidy était considéré comme un artiste bien
sous tous rapports. Le seul vice qu'il se
permettait était de se ronger les ongles.

Fans of the Bay City
Rollers at a concert
in 1974. The
Scottish quintet
were a big hit with
the teenyboppers of
the Seventies.

Fans jubeln den
Bay City Rollers
während eines Kon-
zerts im Jahre 1974
zu. Das schottische
Quintett war bei den
Teenie-Gruppen der
siebziger Jahren
groß in Mode.

Des fans des Bay
City Rollers lors
d'un concert en
1974. Ce groupe
de cinq musiciens
écossais eut beau-
coup de succès
auprès des ado-
lescents des années
soixante-dix.

Reggae singer and songwriter Bob Marley, performing early in his career, in 1973. The big break for Marley and the Wailers came two years later.

Reggae-Sänger und Song-Schreiber Bob Marley bei einem frühen Auftritt im Jahre 1973. Der große Druchbruch kam für Marley und die Wailers zwei Jahre später.

Bob Marley, chanteur reggae et compositeur, sur scène, au début de sa carrière, 1973. La grande percée de Marley et de ses Wailers eut lieu deux ans plus tard.

11-year-old Randy Jackson, Michael's younger brother, braces himself against the winter cold on the London Embankment, November 1972. He stayed in music, but not in the limelight, and in the late Eighties formed a band called Randy and the Gypsies.

Der 11jährige Randy Jackson, jüngerer Bruder von Michael, macht sich auf einen kalten Winter am Ufer Londons gefaßt, November 1972. Er machte Musik, stand aber nicht im Rampenlicht. In den späten achtziger Jahre gründete er die Gruppe Randy and the Gypsies.

Randy Jackson, 11 ans, petit frère de Michael Jackson, s'emmitoufle contre le froid de l'hiver, quai de Londres, novembre 1972. Il continua à faire de la musique, bien qu'on entendît pas beaucoup parler de lui. Il monta un groupe appelé Randy and the Gypsies à la fin des années quatre-vingt.

The American soul funk group Sly and the Family Stone, September 1970 – with Sylvester Stewart, alias Sly Stone (right, front). They had just performed at an Isle of Wight Festival that lost nearly £100,000.

Die amerikanische Soul-Funk-Band Sly and the Family Stone, September 1970 – mit Sylvester Stewart alias Sly Stone (rechts vorn). Kurz zuvor waren sie bei einem Isle-of-Wight-Festival aufgetreten, das mit einem Verlust von fast £ 100.000 endete.

Le groupe américain soul et funk, Sly and the Family Stone, septembre 1970 – avec Sylvester Stewart, alias Sly Stone (devant, à droite). Ils venaient de jouer au festival de l'île de Wight, qui perdit près de 100 000 £.

An exuberant Barry White at a press conference while on tour in March 1977. White was a 'love-god' soul singer and also one of the forerunners of rap, relying a great deal on the spoken rather than the sung word.

Der korpulente Barry White auf einer Pressekonferenz, die er während einer Tournee gab, März 1977. Der begnadete Soulsänger gilt mit seinem Sprechgesang als einer der Vorläufer des Rap.

L'exubérant Barry White lors d'une conférence de presse pendant une tournée en mars 1977. White était un chanteur soul croyant et l'un des précurseurs du rap, chansons parlées plutôt que chantées.

The Three Degrees in a London street, 1974. They were a popular American pop group, featured in the film *The French Connection*.

Die Three Degrees in einer Londoner Straße, 1974. Die populäre amerikanische Popgruppe wirkte in dem Film *Brennpunkt Brooklyn* mit.

Les Three Degrees dans une rue de Londres, 1974. C'était un groupe pop américain populaire qui joua dans le film *French Connection*.

Tina Turner
powering her way
across the stage of
the Hammersmith
Odeon, London,
February 1978, two
years after the split
from Ike.

Tina Turner fegt
über die Bühne
des Hammersmith
Odeon in London,
Februar 1978. Ihre
Trennung von Ike
liegt zwei Jahre
zurück.

Tina Turner, se
propulsant sur la
scène du Hammer-
smith Odeon,
Londres, février
1978, deux ans
après sa séparation
d'avec Ike.

Phil Collins takes
a break, January
1977. Collins was
then vocalist as well
as drummer with
Genesis, following
the departure
of Peter Gabriel.

Phil Collins
während einer
kurzen Pause, Januar
1977. Nach dem
Weggang von Peter
Gabriel wurde
Collins Sänger und
Schlagzeuger der
Gruppe Genesis.

Phil Collins lors
d'une pause, janvier
1977. Collins devint
à la fois chanteur et
percussionniste du
groupe Genesis,
après le départ de
Peter Gabriel.

Mike Oldfield, 1978. In the Seventies, Oldfield made a fortune for himself and the newly formed Virgin Records with 'Tubular Bells'.

Mike Oldfield, 1978. In den siebziger Jahren machte Oldfield ein Vermögen mit den neugegründeten Virgin Records und den „Tubular Bells".

Mike Oldfield, 1978. Dans les années soixante-dix, Oldfield fit, avec « Tubular Bells », sa fortune et celle de la nouvelle maison de disques Virgin Records.

The Seventies pub-rock band Kilburn and the High Roads, with singer, songwriter and founder member Ian Dury (second from left). The photograph was taken by Angela Deale Drummond on 26 November 1974.

Die Kneipenband der siebziger Jahre, Kilburn and the High Roads, mit ihrem Sänger, Song-Schreiber und Mitbegründer Ian Dury (zweiter von links). Angela Deale Drummond nahm dieses Foto am 26. November 1974 auf.

Le groupe pub-rock des années soixante-dix, Kilburn and the High Roads, avec le chanteur, compositeur et membre fondateur Ian Dury (le deuxième à gauche). Photographie d'Angela Deale Drummond, 26 novembre 1974.

The German experimental rock group Can, 1972. (Left to right) Holger Czukay, Michael Karoli, Damo Suzuki, Irmin Schmidt and Jaki Liebezeit. The photograph was taken during their Tago Mago period.

Die deutsche Experimentalrock-Gruppe Can, 1972. (Von links nach rechts) Holger Czukay, Michael Karoli, Damo Suzuki, Irmin Schmidt und Jaki Liebezeit. Das Foto stammt aus ihrer Tago-Mago-Zeit.

Le groupe allemand de rock expérimental Can, 1972. (De gauche à droite) Holger Czukay, Michael Karoli, Damo Suzuki, Irmin Schmidt et Jaki Liebezeit. Photographie prise pendant leur période Tago Mago.

Debbie Harry, London, November 1977. Harry's early career was
adventurous. She left her middle-class background to hang around
with the avant-garde in Greenwich Village, dropped acid, and became
a heroin addict and a groupie before joining Blondie.

Debbie Harry, London, November 1977. Ihre frühe Karriere war
abenteuerlich. Ihrem bürgerlichen Elternhaus kehrte sie den Rücken,
um mit Avantgarde-Künstlern in Greenwich Village herumzuhängen.
Sie nahm LSD, wurde heroinsüchtig und zog als Groupie durchs Land,
bevor sie sich der Gruppe Blondie anschloß.

Debbie Harry, Londres, novembre 1977. Sa carrière précoce fut
aventureuse. Elle quitta son milieu bourgeois pour fréquenter l'avant-
garde de Greenwich Village, laissa tomber le LSD pour l'héroïne et
devint groupie avant de rejoindre Blondie.

London, 1977.
Declan MacManus,
better known
as Elvis Costello,
poses with his
Fender guitar.

London, 1977.
Declan MacManus,
besser bekannt als
Elvis Costello, mit
seiner Fender-
Gitarre.

Londres, 1977.
Declan MacManus,
plus connu sous
le nom d'Elvis
Costello, pose avec
sa guitare Fender.

Shane MacGowan, 19-year-old editor of the punk
rock fanzine *Bondage*, in his office at St Andrews
Chambers, Wells Street, London, January 1977.

Der 19jährige Shane MacGowan war Herausgeber
des Punkrock-Blattes *Bondage*. Hier sitzt er in seinem
Büro der St. Andrews Chambers, Wells Street,
London, Januar 1977.

Shane MacGowan, 19ans, éditeur du magazine de fans
punk rock *Bondage*, dans son bureau à St. Andrews
Chambers, Wells Street, Londres, janvier 1977.

The Sex Pistols, December 1976. (From left to right) Steve Jones, Glen Matlock, Johnny Rotten (John Lydon) and Paul Cook. They had just reduced an interview on a TV show to a string of obscenities. Within days, three-quarters of their gigs were cancelled.

Die Sex Pistols, Dezember 1976. (Von links nach rechts) Steve Jones, Glen Matlock, Johnny Rotten (John Lydon) und Paul Cook. Sie hatten gerade ein Interview in einer Fernsehsendung auf eine Aneinanderreihung von Obszönitäten reduziert. Innerhalb von wenigen Tagen wurden dreiviertel ihrer Auftritte gestrichen.

Les Sex Pistols, décembre 1976. (De gauche à droite) Steve Jones, Glen Matlock, Johnny Rotten (John Lydon) et Paul Cook. Ils venaient de réduire à une suite d'obscénités une interview à la télévision. En l'espace de quelques jours, les troisquarts de leurs concerts furent annulés.

8. Fashion
Mode
La mode

London, November 1973. Janni Goss and Clove Brown model a pair of corduroy jackets with matching caps. Straw, wool (especially crocheted), felt and corduroy were much favoured materials for headgear.

London, November 1973. Die Models Janni Goss und Clove Brown führen Kordsamtjacken mit den dazu passenden Kappen vor. Kopfbedeckungen aus Stroh, Wolle (insbesondere, wenn sie gehäkelt waren), Filz und Kordsamt galten in den siebziger Jahren als der letzte Schrei.

Londres, novembre 1973. Les mannequins Janni Goss et Clove Brown portent des vestes en velours côtelé aux casquettes assorties. La paille, la laine (en particulier crochetée), le feutre et le velours côtelé étaient très à la mode pour la confection des chapeaux.

8. Fashion
  Mode
  La mode

The freedom that had taken root in the Swinging Sixties burst forth in the Seventies. Nothing was too short, too low, too colourful, too overwhelmingly patterned. Women decked themselves out with a splendour to rival birds of paradise. Men strutted like peacocks and popinjays. All the rules were broken. Style bordered on the deformed, with exaggerations of every component: lapels, cuffs, sleeves, hems, ties, collars…

Though the old-established houses of fashion were of course still prolific and profitable, the spotlight turned dazzlingly on younger designers. Yves St Laurent and Mary Quant pursued the trends they had established in the previous decade. Calvin Klein, in his late twenties, became a new major figure on the fashion scene. Vivienne Westwood gained instant fame.

There was a summery softness about many designs. Flowers seemed 'de rigueur'. There was an almost Victorian air of overdecoration, though there was nothing old-fashioned about the way the mini crept higher and higher. Hats were 'in' – not since the Thirties had so many women succumbed to cloche, beret and the wide-brimmed extravaganza.

Evening wear was a riot. Leisure wear was sportingly outrageous. Boots were high and handsome. And, just for once, people seemed actually to like the clothes they wore.

Die Freiheiten der sechziger Jahre brachen in den siebziger Jahren vollends auf. Nichts war zu kurz, zu knapp, zu bunt oder zu stark gemustert. Frauen putzten sich mit einer Pracht heraus, die derjenigen von Paradiesvögeln Konkurrenz machte. Männer stolzierten wie Pfauen und Gecken auf den Straßen. Sämtliche Regeln wurden gebrochen. Stil bedeutete Deformierung, alles wurde übertrieben: Revers, Manschetten, Ärmel, Aufschläge, Krawatten, Kragen …

Etablierte Modehäuser produzierten immer noch kräftig und machten Gewinne, doch im Rampenlicht standen jetzt junge Modedesigner. Yves St. Laurent und Mary Quant setzten den Stil durch, für den sie bereits in den sechziger Jahren den Weg gebahnt hatten. Calvin Klein wurde mit seinen knapp 30 Jahren zu einer gefeierten Figur in der Modewelt. Vivienne Westwood hatte unmittelbar Erfolg.

Im Design herrschte der weiche Stil vor. Blumenmuster waren ein „Muß". Es gab einen fast viktorianischen Hang zur Überdekoration. Doch das war die einzige Reminiszenz an die alte Zeit, denn die Rocksäume rutschten höher und höher. Hüte waren wieder in Mode – seit den dreißiger Jahren hatten Frauen nicht mehr so viele Topfhüte, Baskenmützen und besonders breitkrempige Exemplare getragen.

Die Abendgarderobe löste geradezu Skandale aus. Die Freizeitkleidung war ausgefallen sportlich. Die Stiefel bedeckten das Knie. Und ausnahmsweise fühlten sich die Menschen sichtlich wohl in dem, was sie trugen.

Le vent de liberté qui avait commencé à souffler dans les années soixante se poursuivit tout au long des années soixante-dix. Rien n'était trop court, trop mauvais, trop coloré, trop voyant. Les femmes se paraient de couleurs bigarrées, rivalisant avec les oiseaux de paradis. Les hommes se pavanaient, tels des paons et des perroquets. Toutes les règles étaient abolies. Le style frisait le difforme, exagérant chaque détail : les revers, les poignets des chemises, les manches, les ourlets, les cravates, les cols …

Evidemment, les maisons de couture établies demeurèrent prolifiques et lucratives, mais les projecteurs se tournèrent vers les jeunes créateurs. Yves Saint-Laurent et Mary Quant poursuivirent les tendances qu'ils avaient lancées dans la décennie précédente. Calvin Klein, qui approchait alors la trentaine, devint un personnage important de la mode. Vivienne Westwood eut un succès immédiat.

La douceur estivale était en vogue. Les fleurs étaient de rigueur. Il flottait presque un air de décoration victorienne excessive, bien qu'il n'y eût rien de démodé dans la façon dont la minijupe ne cessait de raccourcir. Les chapeaux étaient revenus à la mode – on n'avait pas vu depuis les années trente autant de femmes succomber aux cloches, aux bérets et à l'excentricité.

Porter des habits de soirée relevait du scandale. Les vêtements de sport étaient arborés avec une décontraction outrageante. Les bottes se portaient hautes. Et, pour une fois, les gens semblaient vraiment aimer les vêtements qu'ils avaient sur le dos.

Russian model Galina Milovskaya in a metallic ensemble with a red fox-fur jacket. In the background is the Vostok space rocket.

Das russische Model Galina Milowskaja präsentiert ein metallisch leuchtendes Ensemble mit roter Fuchsfelljacke. Im Hintergrund ist die Wostok-Weltraumrakete zu sehen.

Le mannequin russe Galina Milovskaya dans un ensemble métallisé et une veste de renard rouge. Derrière elle, la fusée spatiale Vostok.

August 1972.
A classic and classy
piece of Seventies
styling – white satin
trousers with high-
heeled clogs.

August 1972.
Ein Klassiker mit
Klasse aus den
siebziger Jahren –
weiße Satinhose mit
breitem Schlag und
hochhackigen,
offenen Schuhen.

Août 1972.
Tenue classique et
« classe » des années
soixante-dix – le
pantalon en satin
blanc et les galoches
à talon haut.

The mini and the high-heeled platform boots belong to the Seventies. The look on the face of the young man belongs to eternity.

Das Markenzeichen der siebziger Jahre sind Minirock und Stiefel mit hohen Absätzen und Plateausohlen. Der Blick des Herrn im Hintergrund ist dagegen zeitlos.

La minijupe et les bottes à hauts talons et à semelles compensées font partie intégrante des années soixante-dix. L'expression du jeune homme, elle, est intemporelle.

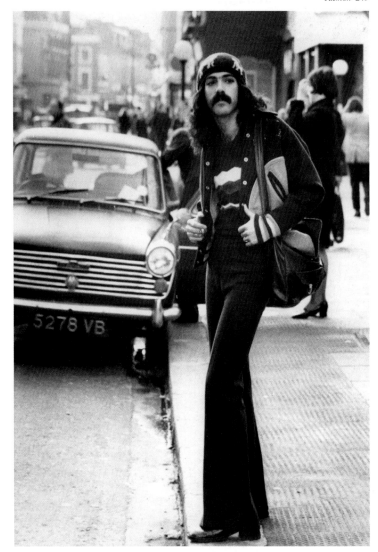

An American hippy, 1972. Dig the knitted skullcap and the freewheeling flared trousers.

Ein amerikanischer Hippie, 1972. Ge-häkeltes Käppi und breite Schlaghosen.

Un hippy américain, 1972. Visez la calotte en tricot et les pantalons à pattes d'éléphant.

Luxury knitwear designed by John Bates is flamboyantly paraded by Marie along a London street, 1974.

Dises edle Strick-Ensemble von John Bates stellt Marie auf elegante Art in einer Londoner Straße vor, 1974.

Un ensemble de luxe en tricot dessiné par John Bates est présenté de façon éclatante par Marie, dans une rue de Londres, 1974.

November 1971.
A lollipop and
deckchair-striped
halter top and
trousers from the
Mary Quant spring
wear collection.

November 1971.
Eine knallige Kom-
bination aus Mary
Quants Frühjahrs-
kollektion: Hose
und rückenfreies
Top mit bunten
Ringelstreifen.

Novembre 1971.
Dos nu et pantalon,
rayés horizontale-
ment et couleur
bonbon, de la col-
lection de printemps
de Mary Quant.

May 1971. A hand-knitted jumpsuit in red and white, and outsize white boots by the young designer Kansai Yamamoto of Tokyo.

Mai 1971. Der junge japanische Designer Kansai Yamamoto aus Tokio entwarf diesen handgestrickten, rot-weißen Einteiler und die übergroßen weißen Stiefel.

Mai 1971. Combinaison en tricot rouge et blanc et bottes blanches de taille exceptionnelle du jeune couturier Kansai Yamamoto de Tokyo.

The T-shirt could come from any age, the slogan is typical Seventies.

Das T-Shirt ist zeitlos, doch der Spruch ist typisch für die siebziger Jahre.

Le T-shirt pourrait être de n'importe quelle époque, le slogan, lui, est typique des années soixante-dix.

British actor
Peter Wyngarde,
September 1970.
Note the cuffs, the
large collars on the
shirt, and the cravat.

Der englische
Schauspieler Peter
Wyngarde, Sep-
tember 1970. Be-
merkenswert sind
die aufgeschlagenen
Manschetten, der
große Hemdkragen
und das Halstuch.

L'acteur britannique
Peter Wyngarde,
septembre 1970.
Notez les manchet-
tes, la cravate et le
col large débordant
sur la veste.

It could be Betty
Grable in the
Forties, but in the
Seventies these high-
cut shorts were
called 'hot pants'
and were thoroughly
modern.

Es könnte Betty
Grable aus den
vierziger Jahren sein,
doch diese knappen
Höschen nannte
man Hot Pants und
galten in den sieb-
ziger Jahren als der
letzte Schrei.

Ce pourrait être
Betty Grable dans
les années quarante,
mais ces shorts
échancrés très haut
étaient appelés « hot
pants » et parfaite-
ment à la mode dans
les années soixante-
dix.

April 1972. A model with an outfit from the Knitwear Fashion Group Show, London. The striped socks are typical of the time.

April 1972. Ein Model präsentiert ein Ensemble der Londoner Strickmodenschau. Die Ringelstrümpfe sind typisch für diese Zeit.

Avril 1972. Un mannequin portant un ensemble du groupe de la mode en tricot, Londres. Les chaussettes rayées sont typiques de cette époque.

London, September 1971.
A denim vest and
enormously flared trouser
combination.

London, September 1971.
Eine Jeanskombination mit
enganliegender Weste und
Hose mit ultraweitem
Schlag.

Londres, septembre 1971.
Un gilet en jean, assorti
d'un pantalon à pattes
d'éléphant très larges.

Two pictures from
a day in St Tropez,
12 June 1972.
The ubiquitous
flared trousers and
a halter top…

Zwei Aufnahmen
aus St. Tropez,
12. Juni 1972. Die
allgegenwärtigen
Hosen mit breitem
Schlag und ein
trägerloses Top …

Deux photos prises
le même jour à
Saint-Tropez, 12 juin
1972. Les pantalons
à pattes d'éléphant
que l'on rencontrait
partout, dos nu …

...and gingham platform shoes, spotted T-shirt and jeans rolled to the knee. 'Roll out those lazy, hazy, crazy days of summer...'

... und offene Schuhe mit Plateausohle, getupftes T-Shirt und bis zu den Knien aufgekrempelte Jeans. „Genieße diese müden, diesigen, verrückten Sommertage ..."

... et des chaussures en vichy à semelles compensées, un T-shirt à pois et des jeans roulés jusqu'aux genoux. « A nous les journées d'été paresseuses, nébuleuses et folles ... »

Coats made from the furs of a variety of felines are modelled in a London street, 1972. In the days before animal rights became an issue, such provocative behaviour passed almost unnoticed.

Bevor Tierschutz ein Thema wurde, störte sich niemand an Pelzmänteln aus dem Fell von allen möglichen Raubkatzen, die wie hier in einer Straße in London 1972 provokativ zur Schau gestellt werden.

Des manteaux fabriqués de fourrure de plusieurs variétés de félins, dans une rue de Londres, 1972. Durant cette période, les droits des animaux n'intéressaient pas encore beaucoup l'opinion et cette conduite provocatrice passait complètement inaperçue.

A white astrakhan cape, fringed with fox tails, designed by Frederick Castet for the Christian Dior Winter Collection, March 1976.

Den weißen Astrachan-Überwurf mit Fuchsschwänzen entwarf Frederick Castet für die Winterkollektion von Christian Dior, März 1976.

Une cape en astrakan blanc, bordée de queues de renard, dessinée par Frederick Castet pour la collection d'hiver de Christian Dior, mars 1976.

The young designer Vivienne Westwood (left), and Malcolm MacLaren (right) outside Bow Street Magistrates Court, London, August 1977.

Die jungen Mode-designer Vivienne Westwood (links) und Malcolm MacLaren (rechts) in der Bow Street vor dem Strafgerichts-hof, London, August 1977.

Les jeunes créateurs de mode, Vivienne Westwood (à gauche) et Malcolm MacLaren (à droite), devant la Cour des magistrats, Bow Street, Londres, août 1977.

Westwood and
MacLaren were the
leading creators
of punk clothing,
but their use of
rubber, leather and
bondage gear led
to a charge of breach
of the peace.

Westwood und
MacLaren gehörten
zu den führenden
Modeschöpfern der
Punk-Mode. Doch
ihre Vorliebe für
Gummi, Leder und
Fesseln empfanden
viele als Übertretung
des guten
Geschmacks.

Westwood et
MacLaren étaient
alors les créateurs de
mode punk les plus
en vue. Mais l'utili-
sation du caout-
chouc, du cuir et
leurs accoutre-ments
d'esclave leur valu-
rent une inculpation
pour atteinte aux
bonnes mœurs.

9. Youth
Die Jugend
La jeunesse

Stockholm, June 1977. A punk rock fan impassively enjoys a concert by the British band, The Clash. Mick Jones, guitarist with The Clash, referred to 'gigs' as 'hostilities', and often the audience adopted a similar attitude.

Stockholm, Juni 1977. Ein Punkrock-Fan genießt gelassen ein Konzert der englischen Band The Clash. Für den Gitarristen der Gruppe, Mick Jones, waren Auftritte ein „Akt der Feindseligkeit". Das Publikum nahm häufig eine ähnliche Haltung ein.

Stockholm, juin 1977. Une fan punk rock savoure, impassible, un concert du groupe britannique The Clash. Mick Jones, guitariste de ce groupe, parlait des concerts comme s'il s'agissait d'« hostilités » et le public adopta souvent une attitude similaire.

9. Youth
Die Jugend
La jeunesse

Shortly before she died in 1971, the French couturier Coco Chanel remarked: 'Youth is something very new: 20 years ago no one mentioned it'.

By the Seventies youth had discovered just how powerful a section of society it was. Its new-found financial clout made it highly influential in fashion, consumerism and pop, where it reigned supreme. It seemed to some that whatever youth wanted was made instantly available.

And what young people wanted was a whole range of new phenomena. They wanted pop festivals. From Woodstock to the Isle of Wight, for three or four days at a time, muddy fields became Utopia. All it took to make the transformation was a stage, an ear-splitting amplification system, hot dogs and hamburgers, portable latrines and the chance to 'let it all hang out'.

They also wanted the Pill, that magic tablet which reduced the concept of chastity to something that concerned only the very holy. Once you or your partner were equipped with the Pill, there was no need for the terror of conception to kill sexual desire.

They wanted pot, the non-aggressive drug that produced calm and peace and love.

In short, they wanted what youth has long wanted – sex, drugs and rock 'n' roll.

Kurz vor ihrem Tod im Jahre 1971 stellte die Grande Dame der französischen Mode Coco Chanel fest: „Jugend ist eine neue Erscheinung: Vor 20 Jahren hat sie keiner erwähnt".

In den siebziger Jahren hatten die Jugendlichen entdeckt, wie stark sie als gesellschaftliche Gruppe waren. Durch ihre Finanzkraft wurden sie im Bereich der Mode, der Konsumindustrie und der Popbranche extrem einflußreich, wenn nicht sogar zur stärksten Kraft. Fast schien es so, daß sämtliche Wünsche der Jugend überall und sofort zu haben waren.

Und was die jungen Menschen verlangten, das war eine ganze Reihe völlig neuer Dinge. Pop-Festivals zum Beispiel – von Woodstock bis zur Isle of Wight –, die drei oder vier Tage dauerten, wo sich Schlammfelder vorübergehend in Utopia verwandelten. Alles, was man für diese Verwandlung benötigte, waren eine Bühne, eine ohrenbetäubende Beschallungsanlage, Hot dogs und Hamburger, transportable Toiletten und die Möglichkeit, sich so richtig gehen zu lassen.

Hinzu kam die Pille, jene magische Tablette, die Keuschheit zu etwas machte, das nur die Heiligen betraf. Hatte man die Pille erst einmal in der Tasche, konnte man seine Lust auf Sex ausleben, ohne Angst vor einer ungewollten Schwangerschaft haben zu müssen.

Und schließlich verlangte die Jugend Haschisch, jene harmlose Droge, die für Ruhe, Frieden und Liebe stand.

Um es kurz zu machen: Die Jugend wünschte sich das, wonach sich junge Leute schon immer gesehnt haben – Sex, Drugs and Rock 'n' Roll.

En 1971, peu de temps avant sa mort, la créatrice de mode française Coco Chanel fit cette remarque : « La jeunesse est quelque chose de très nouveau : il y a 20 ans, personne ne s'en préoccupait ».

Durant les années soixante-dix, la jeunesse prit conscience qu'elle occupait une place importante dans la société. Le pouvoir d'achat tout récent qu'elle détenait lui permit d'influencer la mode, la société de consommation et la musique pop. La jeunesse semblait reine. Il semblait à certains que les jeunes obtenaient tout ce qu'ils voulaient.

Les jeunes désiraient toute une série de nouvelles choses. Ils voulaient des festivals de pop. De Woodstock à l'île de Wight, durant trois ou quatre jours, des champs boueux se métamorphosaient en lieu d'utopie. Une scène, de puissants amplis, des hot dogs et de hamburgers, des toilettes portables et une bonne occasion de se défouler suffisaient à opérer le changement.

Ils voulaient aussi la pilule, ce médicament magique qui réduisait le concept de chasteté à un souci de vieux réactionnaire et permettait de vivre librement sa sexualité.

Ils voulaient du hasch, cette drogue douce qui procure calme, « peace and love ».

Bref, ils voulaient ce que la jeunesse désirait depuis longtemps – « sex, drugs and rock'n'roll ».

Hippy fans parade
through the mud
at the Bardney
Pop Festival,
Lincolnshire,
June 1972. Bardney
was a typical festival
venue – a small town
surrounded by
farmland, whose
inhabitants felt they
had been invaded by
aliens.

Hippies stapfen
durch den Matsch
auf dem Pop-Festival
von Bardney in
Lincolnshire, Juni
1972. Bardney war
ein ganz typischer
Ort solcher Festivals
– ein kleines
Provinzstädtchen
inmitten von
Feldern und Wiesen,
dessen Einwohner
glaubten, sie hätten
es mit
Außerirdischen zu
tun.

Parade de fans
hippy dans la
boue, festival pop
de Bardney,
Lincolnshire,
juin 1972. Bardney
était un lieu de
festival typique –
petite ville isolée
dont les habitants
eurent l'impression
d'être envahis par
des extra-terrestres.

Love at the Isle of Wight Pop Festival, August 1970. It was a great success. 600,000 people attended, the stage caught fire, and the promoters lost money.

Liebe auf dem Isle-of-Wight-Festival, August 1970. Das Festival war zwar mit 600.000 Besuchern ein Riesenerfolg, doch als die Bühne Feuer fing, verloren die Veranstalter ihr Geld.

L'amour au festival pop de l'île de Wight, août 1970. Ce festival fut un grand succès. 600 000 personnes y assistèrent, la scène prit feu et les organisateurs perdirent de l'argent.

An icon of Seventies youth (the Vespa scooter) in its ideal setting (the sea front at Brighton on the south coast of England), 1979. The helmet in the background proudly proclaims where one Mod's musical loyalty lay.

Absolut typisch für die Jugend der siebziger Jahre ist die Vespa, hier in geradezu idealer Umgebung (die Küstenpromenade Brightons in Südengland), 1979. Die Aufschrift auf dem Helm im Hintergrund macht deutlich, wem die musikalische Vorliebe der Mods gilt.

Une Vespa, symbole de la jeunesse des années soixante-dix dans un cadre idéal (le bord de mer à Brighton, côte sud de l'Angleterre), 1979. Le casque à l'arrière-plan proclame fièrement la préférence musicale des Mods.

A hippy wedding at the Watchfield Pop
Festival, Oxfordshire, August 1975. David
Beale and June Dyminski, the groom and
bride, are partly hidden by a tambourine
(left). The ceremony was performed by
the Festival organizer Sid Rawle, in the
role of a naked vicar.

Eine Hippie-Hochzeit auf dem Pop-
Festival von Watchfield, Oxfordshire,
August 1975. Der Bräutigam David Beale
und die Braut June Dyminski werden
teilweise von einem Tamburin (links)
verdeckt. Die Zeremonie wurde von dem
Veranstalter Sid Rawle abgehalten,
der hier als nackter Pfarrer auftritt.

Un mariage hippy au festival pop de
Watchfield, Oxfordshire, août 1975. Les
mariés, David Beale et June Dyminski,
sont en partie cachés par un tambourin (à
gauche). La cérémonie fut célébrée par
l'organisateur du festival, Sid Rawle, dans
le rôle du pasteur nu.

A Rocker arrives at the Wembley Rock 'n' Roll Festival on his Honda chopper motorcycle, August 1972.

Ein Rocker trifft auf dem Rock 'n' Roll-Festival von Wembley mit seinem Honda-Chopper ein, August 1972.

Un rocker arrive au festival de rock'n'roll de Wembley sur sa Honda à guidon surélevé, août 1972.

Police are called in to restore order at the Weeley Pop Festival, Essex, when fighting breaks out between the organizers and a chapter of Hell's Angels, August 1971. The Angels did a lot of damage, but were routed by festival vigilantes who destroyed their bikes.

Auf dem Pop-Festival von Weeley, Essex, mußte die Polizei einschreiten, weil es zu Auseinandersetzungen zwischen Mitgliedern der Hell's Angels und den Veranstaltern kam, August 1971. Die Angels richteten allerhand Schaden an, konnten aber schließlich von den Sicherheitskräften des Festivals vertrieben werden, indem sie deren Motorräder demolierten.

La police est appelée pour remettre de l'ordre lors du festival pop de Weeley, Essex, alors que des combats éclatent entre les organisateurs et un groupe de Hell's Angels, août 1971. Les Angels firent beaucoup de dégâts, mais le comité de sécurité détruisit leurs motos et les mit en déroute.

A group of punks and skinheads face eviction from a house in which they had been squatting, 25 June 1979. Thatcherism was just seven weeks old.

Eine Gruppe von Punkern und Skinheads sieht der Zwangsräumung ihres Hauses entgegen, das sie besetzt hatten, 25. Juni 1979. Margaret Thatcher war erst sieben Wochen im Amt.

Un groupe de punks et de skinheads affrontant leur expulsion d'une maison qu'ils squattaient, 25 juin 1979. Le thatchérisme n'avait que sept semaines.

Nobby Clark's portrait of a young man smoking a king-size joint, Hyde Park, London, 1970. There were frequent calls to have marijuana legalized, but it was seen as the first step on the road to heroin addiction, crime or, at least, shiftlessness.

Nobby Clark nahm diesen jungen Mann auf, der im Hyde Park einen gigantischen Joint raucht, London, 1970. Immer wieder wurde die Forderung laut, Marihuana zu legalisieren, doch das Rauschmittel galt als Einstiegsdroge auf dem Weg in die Heroinabhängigkeit, Kriminalität oder, im harmlosesten Fall, in die Lethargie.

Portrait par Nobby Clark d'un jeune homme fumant un joint géant, Hyde Park, Londres, 1970. Nombreux furent ceux qui demandèrent la légalisation de la marijuana ; mais celle-ci était considérée comme le premier pas vers l'héroïne, la criminalité ou, du moins, la paresse.

Pop fans gather beneath the trees of Windsor Great Park, near London, for a 'Free Festival', August 1973. Ignoring the regulations they lit fires with branches from trees and littered the grass with bottles and cans.

Popfans lagern unter den Bäumen des Windsor-Parks in der Nähe von London bei einem „Gratis-Festival", August 1973. Trotz aller Regeln wurden Feuer mit Ästen von Bäumen angezündet und die Grasflächen mit Flaschen und Dosen verschmutzt.

Des fans de musique pop se rassemblent sous les arbres du grand parc de Windsor, près de Londres, pour un « festival libre », août 1973. Ignorant les règlements, ils allumaient des feux avec les branches des arbres et laissaient leurs déchets sur la pelouse.

February 1970. British skinheads outside a pub. When the punks came along, a little later, the general public in Britain didn't know who to hate most – punks or skinheads. Punks did more damage, they reckoned, but skinheads were more violent.

Februar 1970. Englische Skinheads stehen vor der Tür eines Pubs. Als bald auch noch die Punker auftauchten, konnte sich die britische Öffentlichkeit nicht entscheiden, welche Gruppe ihnen verhaßter war. Man glaubte, daß die Punker mehr Schaden anrichteten als die Skinheads, aber letztere waren brutaler.

Février 1970. Des skinheads britanniques devant un pub. Quand les punks arrivèrent un peu plus tard, les Anglais ne savaient trop lesquels des punks ou des skinheads détester le plus. Ils estimèrent que les punks faisaient beaucoup de dégâts, mais que les skinheads étaient plus violents.

Teenage pupils
arrive at the 'trendy'
Holland Park
Comprehensive
School in West
London, October
1971.

Jugendliche Schüle-
rinnen treffen in der
„angesagten" Ge-
samtschule Holland
Park im Westen
Londons ein,
Oktober 1971.

Des adolescentes
arrivent à l'école
secondaire « en
vogue » de Holland
Park, ouest de
Londres, octobre
1971.

Punk rock fans let rip during a concert by two
British bands, The Jam and The Clash, at the
Rainbow Theatre, London, May 1977. Both
bands were then new on the scene.

Punkrock-Fans legen bei einem Konzert der
beiden englischen Gruppen The Jam und The
Clash im Londoner Rainbow Theatre los, Mai
1977. Beide Bands waren neu in der Szene.

Des fans de punk rock se déchaînent lors du
concert de deux groupes britanniques tout
nouveaux sur la scène musicale, The Jam et The
Clash, au Rainbow Theatre, Londres, mai 1977.

A young skinhead in
a pub expresses
his views on life in
body language,
1978. In the end,
the public decided
skinheads were
worse than punks.

Die Körpersprache
dieses Skinheads in
einem Pub drückt
seine Einstellung
zum Leben aus,
1978. Schließlich
stand für die Öffent-
lichkeit doch fest,
daß Skinheads
schlimmer als
Punker seien.

Dans un pub, un
jeune skinhead
exprime en langage
corporel sa concep-
tion de la vie, 1978.
Les gens finirent par
trouver les skinheads
pires que les punks.

Head line… A young fan waits to get in to the Rainbow Theatre, London, for The Jam and The Clash gig, 16 May 1977. Across her forehead is written the forlorn message 'No future'.

Kopfzeile … Ein junger Fan wartet vor dem Londoner Rainbow Theatre auf den Einlaß, es spielten dort The Jam und The Clash, 16. Mai 1977. Auf ihrer Stirn steht der verzweifelte Wahlspruch „No Future".

Titre en tête … Une jeune fan attend de pouvoir entrer dans le Rainbow Theatre, à Londres, pour le concert des groupes The Jam et The Clash, 16 mai 1977. Sur son front, le message désespéré : « No Future ».

...Bottom line.
A young man at the
bar of The Roxy
nightclub, London,
March 1978.
His message reads:
'Bollocks to you all'.

... Fußzeile. Ein
junger Mann steht
am Tresen des
Londoner Nacht-
clubs Roxy, März
1978. Seine Bot-
schaft lautet:
„Scheiß auf Euch
alle".

... Titre au posté-
rieur. Un jeune
homme au bar de la
boîte de nuit The
Roxy, Londres, mars
1978. Son message :
« Des couilles pour
vous tous. »

10. Sport
Sport
Le sport

Wembley, London, April 1978. England striker Kevin Keegan celebrates after scoring a goal against Brazil. It was a friendly match which ended in a 1-1 draw.

Wembley, London, April 1978. Englands Torschütze Kevin Keegan jubelt nach seinem Treffer gegen Brasilien. Das Spiel war eine faire Partie und endete 1:1 unentschieden.

Wembley, Londres, avril 1978. Le buteur anglais, Kevin Keegan, fou de joie, après avoir marqué un but contre le Brésil. Ce fut une partie amicale qui se termina par un match nul, 1:1.

10. Sport
Sport
Le sport

All sports have their golden ages. In the Seventies it was the turn of tennis, as the Grand Slam greats – Connors, McEnroe, Navratilova, King, Evert and Borg – gave fans the most thrilling displays of skill and stamina the world had ever seen.

In football, Brazil (1970), West Germany (1974) and Argentina (1978) took the World Cup, while a young man from Northern Ireland took most of the headlines. His name was George Best. He was phenomenally talented and a lover of life. In the words of one popular newspaper: 'Georgie… floats amid clouds of girls over mountains of money.'

The Americans Lee Trevino and Jack Nicklaus shared most of golf's top honours. Jackie Stewart, Emerson Fittipaldi and Niki Lauda each carried away the Formula One World Championship twice. The powerful West Indies carried all before them on the cricket field, while a series of streakers carried nothing before – or after – them.

Despite the horrors of the killings by members of the Black September movement, the 1972 Munich Olympics were completed as planned. The Soviet gymnast, Olga Korbut, became the darling of the crowds, winning two gold medals and one silver. Four years later, at Montreal, Nadia Comaneci of Romania pushed Korbut into second place.

Jede Sportart hat ihre Glanzzeiten. Die siebziger Jahre waren die große Ära des Tennissports, Grand-Slam-Stars wie Connors, McEnroe, Navratilova, King, Evert und Borg lieferten Spiele voller Spannung und Ausdauer, wie sie die Welt noch nicht gesehen hatte.

Brasilien (1970), Deutschland (1974) und Argentinien (1978) wurden Fußball-Weltmeister, doch die Schlagzeilen wurden von einem jungen Mann aus Nordirland beherrscht: George Best war ein unglaubliches Naturtalent und Lebenskünstler. Eine der populärsten Zeitungen schrieb: „George … schwebt inmitten einer Wolke junger Frauen über Bergen von Geld."

Die US-Amerikaner Lee Trevino und Jack Nicklaus teilten sich die meisten Siege der großen Golfturniere. Jackie Stewart, Emerson Fittipaldi und Niki Lauda wurden jeweils zweimal Weltmeister in der Formel-1. Das starke Team von den westindischen Inseln hatte freie Bahn auf dem Kricketfeld, woran auch eine ganze Reihe von Nacktläufern („Flitzer") nichts ändern konnte.

Trotz der tödlichen Katastrophe, die die Terrorgruppe Schwarzer September während der Olympiade in München 1972 anrichtete, gingen die Spiele wie geplant zu Ende. Die sowjetische Turnerin Olga Korbut eroberte die Herzen der Zuschauer und gewann zwei Gold- und eine Silbermedaille. Vier Jahre später wurde sie in Montreal von der Rumänin Nadia Comaneci auf den zweiten Platz verwiesen.

Tous les sports ont leur âge d'or. Dans les années soixante-dix, ce fut le tour du tennis, quand les héros du Grand Slam – Connors, McEnroe, Navratilova, King, Evert et Borg – offrirent à leurs fans la gamme la plus sensationnelle de talents et d'endurance que le monde ait jamais vue.

En football, le Brésil (1970), l'Allemagne de l'Ouest (1974) et l'Argentine (1978) remportèrent la Coupe du monde, alors qu'un jeune homme d'Irlande du Nord occupait la une des journaux. Il s'appelait George Best. Il était pourvu d'un immense talent et d'un féroce appétit de vivre. Pour reprendre les mots d'un journal populaire : « Georgie … flotte parmi des nuages de filles au-dessus de montagnes d'argent. »

Les Américains Lee Trevino et Jack Nicklaus se partagèrent les palmarès du golf. Jackie Stewart, Emerson Fittipaldi et Niki Lauda remportèrent à deux reprises le Grand Prix de Formule 1. Sur les terrains de cricket, la puissante équipe des Antilles l'emporta sur tous les plans, malgré les provocations intempestives d'une série d'hommes nus.

Malgré l'horrible massacre perpétré par les membres du groupe Septembre noir, les Jeux olympiques de Munich se terminèrent comme prévu. La gymnaste soviétique Olga Korbut était la coqueluche des foules : elle remporta deux médailles d'or et une d'argent. Quatre ans plus tard, à Montréal, Nadia Comaneci de Roumanie la relégua à la seconde place.

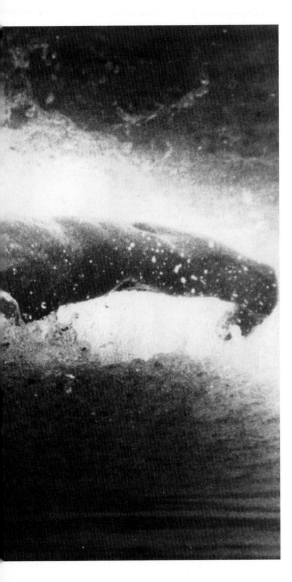

American swimmer Mark Spitz in action during a training session at the Munich Olympics, August 1972. Spitz won a record seven gold medals at Munich. They included the 100 and 200 metres freestyle, and the 100 and 200 metres butterfly.

Der amerikanische Schwimmer Mark Spitz in Aktion bei Wettkampfvorbereitungen während der Münchener Olympiade, August 1972. Spitz gewann in München den Rekord mit sieben Goldmedaillen, unter anderem im 100 und 200 Meter Freistil sowie im 100 und 200 Meter Schmetterling.

Le nageur américain Mark Spitz en pleine action pendant une séance d'entraînement aux Jeux olympiques de Munich, août 1972. Spitz battit un record en remportant sept médailles d'or à Munich, dont celles des 100 et 200 mètres nage libre, ainsi que celles des 100 et 200 mètres papillon.

Martina Navratilova
on her way to
beating her
American team mate
Rosie Casals in
the third round of
the Women's
Singles, Wimbledon,
29 June 1979.
She went on to
become Champion.

Martina Navratilova
auf ihrem Weg zum
Sieg über die ameri-
kanische Teamkol-
legin Rosie Casals in
der dritten Runde
der Dameneinzel,
Wimbledon, 29. Juni
1979. Sie war auf
dem Weg zum
Champion.

Martina Navratilova
sur le point de battre
sa collègue améri-
caine Rosie Casals,
pendant le troisième
set du simple dames,
Wimbledon, 29 juin
1979. Elle était en
train de devenir une
championne.

Tracy Austin, Wimbledon, July 1979. Though she never had much luck at Wimbledon, this was the year in which she won the US Open.

Tracy Austin, Wimbledon, Juli 1979. Obwohl sie in Wimbledon nie Glück hatte, gewann sie im selben Jahr die US Open.

Tracy Austin, Wimbledon, juillet 1979. Bien qu'elle n'eût jamais beaucoup de chance à Wimbledon, ce fut l'année où elle gagna l'US Open.

Ilie Nastase of
Romania, 1978.
He was always
popular with the
crowds, winning the
US Open in 1972
and the French
Open in 1973.

Der Rumäne Ilie
Nastase, 1978. Der
Publikumsliebling
gewann 1972 die US
Open und 1973 die
French Open.

Le roumain Ilie
Nastase, 1978. Il
jouissait d'une
grande popularité et
remporta l'US Open
en 1972 et le tour-
noi de Roland-
Garros en 1973.

Wimbledon, June 1979. Often unpopular with the crowds, John McEnroe holds his nose after disagreeing with a line-judge's call.

Wimbledon, Juni 1979. John McEnroe gehörte nie zu den Publikumslieblingen. Hier kneift er sich die Nase zu, weil er mit einer Entscheidung des Linienrichters unzufrieden ist.

Wimbledon, juin 1979. Souvent impopulaire, John McEnroe se pince le nez avec mépris après un désaccord avec un juge de ligne.

Chris Evert at Wimbledon, June 1973.
The following year she became Wimbledon
champion, and subsequently she won the US
Open four years running, from 1975 to 1978.

Chris Evert in Wimbledon, Juni 1973. Im darauffolgenden Jahr gewann sie Wimbledon und siegte
darauf vier Jahre hintereinander, von 1975 bis
1978, bei den US Open.

Chris Evert, Wimbledon, juin 1973. Elle devint
championne de Wimbledon l'année suivante et
remporta quatre années de suite l'US Open, de
1975 à 1978.

Wimbledon, 6 July 1974. US tennis stars Jimmy Connors (winner of the Men's Singles) and Chris Evert (winner of the Women's Singles) show their trophies to fans – one of whom is a Borg look-alike.

Wimbledon, 6. Juli 1974. Die amerikanischen Tennisstars Jimmy Connors (Sieger im Herreneinzel) und Chris Evert (Siegerin im Dameneinzel) präsentieren ihre Trophäen den Fans – von denen einer Björn Borg sehr ähnlich sieht.

Wimbledon, 6 juillet 1974. La star de tennis américaine Jimmy Connors (vainqueur du simple messieurs) et Chris Evert (qui avait remporté le simple dames) font admirer leurs trophées à des fans – dont l'un d'entre eux ressemble étrangement à Borg.

Rome, March 1970. Inter Milan centre forward Pino Boninsegna leaps over
Lazio's Giorgio Papadopulo during their match at the Olympic Stadium. On
the left is Milan's Giacinto Facchetti, and on the right Lazio's goalkeeper,
Rosario di Vencenzo.

Rom, März 1970. Während des Spiels im Olympiastadion springt der
Mittelstürmer von Inter Mailand, Pino Boninsegna, über Giorgio Papadopulo
von Lazio Rom. Links im Bild sein Mannschaftskollege Giacinto Facchetti und
rechts der Torhüter von Lazio Rom, Rosario di Vencenzo.

Rome, mars 1970. L'avant-centre de l'Inter Milan, Pino Boninsegna, bondit
par-dessus le joueur Giorgio Papadopulo du Lazio durant le match au stade
olympique. A gauche se trouve Giacinto Facchetti de Milan et, à droite, le
gardien de but du Lazio, Rosario di Vencenzo.

Johan Cruyff, 1972.
Cruyff was
European Foot-
baller of the Year in
1973 and 1974, and
captain of the Dutch
team that lost the
World Cup Final in
1974.

Johan Cruyff, 1972.
Der Kapitän der
holländischen
Mannschaft war
1973 und 1974
europäischer Fuß-
baller des Jahres.
Doch im Endspiel
der Fußballwelt-
meisterschaft von
1974 verlor das
holländische Team.

Johan Cruyff, 1972.
Cruyff fut élu foot-
balleur européen de
l'année en 1973 et
1974 et fut le capi-
taine de l'équipe
hollandaise qui
perdit en finale de
la Coupe du monde
en 1974.

The Brazilian soccer star, Edson Arantes do Nascimento, better known as Pelé, holds the World Cup aloft, Paris, 31 March 1971. Brazil had won the Cup in 1970.

Der brasilianische Fußballstar Edson Arantes do Nascimento, Pelé genannt, streckt den Weltpokal empor, Paris, 31. März 1971. Brasilien hatte die Fußballweltmeisterschaft 1970 gewonnen.

Le joueur de football brésilien, Edson Arantes do Nascimento, plus connu sous le nom de Pelé, brandit la Coupe du monde, Paris, 31 mars 1971. Le Brésil avait remporté la Coupe en 1970.

West German goalkeeper Sepp Maier balances the World Cup on his head after West Germany's 2-1 defeat of Holland in the final, Munich, 1974.

Deutschlands Torhüter Sepp Maier balanciert den Pokal auf seinem Kopf. Das deutsche Team hatte die Holländer im Endspiel der Fußballweltmeisterschaft in München 2:1 geschlagen, 1974.

Le gardien de but ouest-allemand, Sepp Maier, pose la Coupe du monde sur sa tête après la victoire par 2:1 de l'Allemagne de l'Ouest sur la Hollande, Munich, 1974.

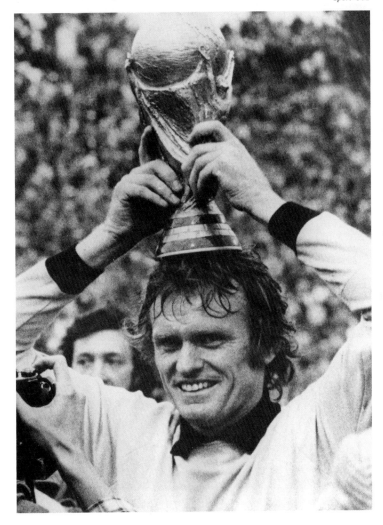

London, October
1975. 19-year-old
Olga Korbut of the
Soviet Union trains
for the Gymnastics
World Cup,
Wembley Arena.

London, Oktober
1975. Die 19jährige
Olga Korbut aus der
Sowjetunion
trainiert für die
Weltmeisterschaften
im Kunstturnen in
der Sporthalle
von Wembley.

Londres, octobre
1975. La Soviétique
Olga Korbut, 19 ans,
s'entraîne dans le
stade de Wembley
pour la Coupe du
monde de
gymnastique.

Romanian gymnast
Nadia Comaneci
performs on the
balance beam at the
Montreal Olympics,
21 July 1976. She
obtained her fourth
perfect score.

Die rumänische
Turnerin Nadia
Comaneci zeigt ihr
Können auf dem
Schwebebalken,
Olympiade in
Montreal, 21. Juli
1976. Sie erhält ihre
vierte Bestnote.

La gymnaste
roumaine Nadia
Comaneci, lors
d'une acrobatie sur
poutre, durant les
Jeux olympiques de
Montréal, 21 juillet
1976. Elle obtint
pour la quatrième
fois la note
maximale.

Joe Frazier, Madison Square Garden, New York City, March 1971. Frazier beat
Muhammad Ali on points and retained his Heavyweight Championship. The fight was
so thrilling that one member of the crowd died of a heart attack.

Joe Frazier im New Yorker Madison Square Garden, März 1971. Frazier besiegte
Muhammad Ali nach Punkten und blieb damit Weltmeister im Schwergewicht. Der
Kampf war so spannend, daß einer der Zuschauer einen Herzinfarkt erlitt und starb.

Joe Frazier, Madison Square Garden, New York, mars 1971. Frazier battit Mohammed
Ali aux points et conserva son titre de champion du monde poids lourds. Ce combat fut
si palpitant qu'un spectateur mourut d'une crise cardiaque.

Muhammad Ali, 1970. It was the year in which he was reinstated as World Heavyweight Champion by the Supreme Court of the United States. Ali had been stripped of the title for refusing military service in 1967.

Muhammad Ali, 1970. In jenem Jahr erkannte der Oberste Gerichtshof der Vereinigten Staaten seinen Weltmeistertitel im Schwergewicht wieder an, der ihm abgesprochen worden war, weil er 1967 den Militärdienst verweigert hatte.

Mohammed Ali, 1970. Cette année-là, la Cour suprême des Etats-Unis lui rendit son titre de champion du monde poids lourds. Il en avait été dépouillé en 1967 après avoir refusé de faire son service militaire.

July 1979. Muhammad Ali indulges in a little street fighting. Ali dominated the boxing world in the Seventies. He twice lost, and twice regained, his World Championship title.

Juli 1979. Muhammad Ali wird in einen kleinen Straßenkampf verwickelt. Ali beherrschte die Box-Szene der siebziger Jahre. Der Schwergewichtler verlor zweimal den Weltmeistertitel und holte ihn sich zweimal wieder zurück.

Juillet 1979. Mohammed Ali se laisse aller à un simulacre de combat dans la rue. Ali fut le personnage dominant du monde de la boxe des années soixante-dix. Il perdit deux fois son titre de champion du monde et le regagna deux fois.

Rumble in the Jungle, October 1974. Muhammad Ali with President Mobutu Sese Seko of Zaire. A few hours later, Ali knocked out George Foreman in spectacular fashion to became Heavyweight Champion.

Aufruhr im Dschungel, Oktober 1974. Muhammad Ali mit Präsident Mobutu Sese Seko aus Zaire. Einige Stunden später schlug Ali sensationell George Foreman k. o. und wurde Weltmeister im Schwergewicht.

Péripéties en prévision, octobre 1974. Mohammed Ali avec le président Mobutu Sese Seko du Zaïre. Quelques heures plus tard, Ali mettait George Foreman K.-O. d'une manière spectaculaire, et ainsi devenait champion en poids lourd.

Belgian cyclist Eddie Merckx wins the World Professional Road
Championship at Mendrisio, Switzerland, 7 September 1971. Merckx
won the Tour de France four times in the Seventies.

Der belgische Radrennfahrer Eddie Merckx gewinnt den
Weltmeistertitel im Straßenrennen der Profis in Mendrisio, Schweiz,
7. September 1971. In den siebziger Jahren gewann Merckx die Tour
de France viermal.

Le cycliste belge Eddie Merckx remporte le championnat de cyclisme
professionnel sur route à Mendrisio, Suisse, 7 septembre 1971.
Merckx fut quatre fois vainqueur du Tour de France dans les années
soixante-dix.

In the shadow of Ali… British boxer Joe Bugner trains for his fight with Richard Dunn, London, September 1976.

Im Schatten von Ali … Der englische Boxer Joe Bugner trainiert für seinen Kampf gegen Richard Dunn, London, September 1976.

Dans l'ombre d'Ali … Le boxeur britannique Joe Bugner s'entraîne pour son combat contre Richard Dunn, Londres, septembre 1976.

Lasse Viren, Montreal, July 1976. Viren won the 5,000 and 10,000 metres at both the Munich and Montreal Olympics.

Lasse Viren in Montreal, Juli 1976. Er gewann bei den Olympischen Spielen von München und Montreal die 5.000- und 10.000-Meter-Läufe.

Lasse Viren, Montréal, juillet 1976. Viren remporta les 5 000 et 10 000 mètres aux Jeux olympiques de Munich et de Montréal.

What matters is taking part… James Owens competes in the 110 metres hurdles final at the Montreal Olympics, July 1976. The gold medal went to Guy Drut of France.

Dabei sein ist alles … James Owens kämpft um den Sieg im 110-Meter-Hürden-Finale bei der Olympiade in Montreal, Juli 1976. Die Goldmedaille ging an den Franzosen Guy Drut.

L'important, c'est de participer … James Owens sur le parcours de la finale du 110 mètres haies lors des Jeux olympiques de Montréal, juillet 1976. Le français Guy Drut remporta la médaille d'or.

Lester Piggott leads the 2,000 Guineas winner,
Nijinsky, through the crowds at Newmarket
Racecourse, 29 April 1970. Six weeks later, the
same horse and rider won the Derby at Epsom.

Lester Piggott führt Nijinsky, das Rennpferd
hat schon 2.000 Guineas Preisgelder
gewonnen, durch die Menge auf der Renn-
bahn von Newmarket, 29. April 1970. Sechs
Wochen später gewinnen Reiter und Pferd
auch das Derby in Epsom.

Lester Piggott mène Nijinsky, le cheval qui
vient de gagner 2 000 guinées, à travers la
foule du champ de courses de Newmarket,
29 avril 1970. Six semaines plus tard, cheval
et jockey gagneront le derby d'Epsom.

Red Rum clears a fence
at Haydock Park,
February 1973. Red
Rum was a bookies'
nightmare, winning the
Grand National in
1973, 1974 and 1977.

Red Rum nimmt ein
Hindernis im Haydock
Park, Februar 1973.
Das Pferd war der Alp-
traum aller Wettbüros,
es gewann den Grand
National 1973, 1974
und 1977.

Red Rum franchissant
un obstacle à Haydock
Park, février 1973. Il
était le cauchemar des
bookmakers, il remporta
le Grand National en
1973, 1974 et 1977.

West Indian cricket supporters, Kennington
Oval, London, August 1976. They were
happy because they were watching their team
beat England by an innings and 231 runs.

Westindische Kricketfans, Kennington Oval,
London, August 1976. Sie hatten allen Grund
zum Jubeln, denn ihr Team siegte über
England mit einer Runde und 231 Läufen.

Des supporters de l'équipe de cricket des
Antilles, Kennington Oval, Londres, août 1976.
Fous de joie, ils regardaient leur équipe battre
l'Angleterre par un tour de batte et 231 points.

'The tribe that lost its head…' Scottish football fans invade the pitch, Wembley Stadium, London, 4 June 1977. They were happy because their team had just defeated England by two goals to one, and because they'd had a wee dram or three.

„Die Fans waren nicht mehr zu halten …" Schottische Fußballfans stürmen das Spielfeld im Londoner Wembley-Stadion, 4. Juni 1977. Sie waren glücklich, weil ihre Mannschaft das englische Team 2:1 geschlagen hatte und weil sie sicher das eine oder andere Glas zuviel getrunken hatten.

« La tribu qui perdit la tête … » Des fans de football écossais envahissent le stade de Wembley, Londres, 4 juin 1977. Ils sont heureux parce que leur équipe vient tout juste de battre l'Angleterre par deux buts à un et qu'ils ont bu un petit verre de trop.

Australian captain Greg Chappell does the decent thing in a World Series game against the West Indies, Brisbane, Australia, December 1979.

Der australische Mannschaftskapitän Greg Chappell macht das, was er in den Weltmeisterschaftsspielen gegen die westindische Mannschaft in Brisbane, Australien, für anständig hält, Dezember 1979.

Le capitaine australien Greg Chappell obéit aux convenances lors de la Coupe du monde contre les Antilles, Brisbane, Australie, décembre 1979.

Just not cricket…
A streaker vaults
over the stumps at
Lord's cricket
ground, London,
September 1976.

Alles andere als
Kricket … Ein
„Flitzer" schwingt
sich über ein Tor auf
dem Lord's cricket
ground in London,
September 1976.

Tout sauf du cricket
… Un provocateur
nu saute par-dessus
les piquets, sur le
terrain de Lord's
cricket ground
Londres, septembre
1976.

The closing ceremony at
the Montreal Olympics,
Canada, August 1976. The
dance display by scores of
young women is disturbed
by a lone streaker (centre
right). The man was
arrested by the Canadian
Mounted Police.

Die Schlußzeremonie
der Olympischen Spiele
von Montreal, Kanada,
August 1976. Die
Tanzvorführung einiger
hundert junger Frauen wird
von einem vereinzelten
„Flitzer" (Mitte rechts)
gestört. Der Mann
wurde von der berittenen
kanadischen Polizei fest-
genommen.

Cérémonie de clôture
des Jeux olympiques
de Montréal, Canada,
août 1976. Un provocateur
nu isolé (au centre, à droite)
chamboule la chorégraphie
de plusieurs jeunes femmes.
Il fut arrêté par la police
montée canadienne.

A woman ski acrobat performs a salto with cross-skis during a competition at Laax, Switzerland, 1977.

Eine Skiakrobatin führt bei einem Wettkampf im Schweizer Wintersportort Laax einen Salto mit über Kreuz gestellten Skiern vor, 1977.

Une acrobate de ski effectue un salto avec skis croisés, lors d'une compétition à Laax, Suisse, 1977.

John Curry, British
ice skater, rehearses
for an ice show
in 1976 – the year
in which he won
the European,
World and Olympic
figure-skating
championships.

Der englische Eis-
kunstläufer John
Curry probt für eine
Eisrevue im Jahre
1976 – das Jahr, in
dem er die Europa-,
die Welt- und die
Olympiameister-
schaft im Eiskunst-
laufen gewann.

John Curry, patineur
sur glace britanni-
que, s'entraîne en
1976 pour un
spectacle sur glace –
l'année où il rem-
porta les champion-
nats européen, mon-
dial et olympique de
patinage artistique.

11. Children
Kinder
Les enfants

London, 1971. Not waifs or strays, but two very middle-class children
model clothes from the New Children's Wonder Boutique
in Hampstead. The boy's fleecy jacket and the girl's smock are
probably miniature versions of their parents' clothes.

London, 1971. Dies sind keine obdachlosen Kinder, sondern zwei
typische Mittelstandssprößlinge, die Kindermode aus der New
Children's Wonder Boutique aus Hampstead vorführen. Die
Zottelfellweste des kleinen Jungen und das Kleid des Mädchens
sind vermutlich die Miniaturausgaben der elterlichen Garderobe.

Londres, 1971. Non, ce ne sont pas deux enfants abandonnés, mais
des enfants de la bonne bourgeoisie, posant pour les vêtements de la
boutique New Children's Wonder à Hampstead. Le gilet moutonné du
jeune garçon, ainsi que les smocks de la robe de la petite fille, sont
probablement des versions miniatures des habits de leurs parents.

11. Children
Kinder
Les enfants

Adults like to invest the concept of childhood with an aura of magic. They like to see it as a land where a stick can be a sword or a trumpet, a wood can be a castle, a packing case a Ferrari – and when all it takes to make dreams come true is sunshine and time.

It became increasingly difficult for adults to maintain these fantasies in the Seventies. Under the saturated world surveillance provided by television cameras, childhood pains and sorrows came to the fore.

In the West, schoolchildren organized themselves into unions, and challenged the authorities on everything from punishments to uniforms. There were reports of 10-year-olds opening bank accounts, of parents being openly accused of cruelty or inadequacy by their offspring. Little innocents were becoming worldly-wise.

All this was nothing compared with the shattering stories that came from Africa, South America, China and the Far East. Adults learnt of vast swathes of the planet where children were starving to death in their millions, of places where children went to war at the age of six, of child labour and child prostitution.

And yet, somehow, for the lucky few, there was still enough sunshine and enough time.

Erwachsene lieben es, die kindliche Welt mit einer Aura des Magischen zu umgeben. Für sie ist es ein Land, wo ein Stock zu einem Schwert oder einer Trompete werden kann, ein Stück Holz zu einer Burg und eine Schachtel zu einem Ferrari – und wo man nur Sonnenschein und Zeit braucht, um diese Träume zu verwirklichen.

Doch in den siebziger Jahren wurde es für die Erwachsenen immer schwieriger, diese Phantasiewelten zu bewahren. Durch die mittlerweile allgegenwärtige Bilderflut der Fernsehkameras konnte man am Kummer und Leid so vieler Kinder nicht mehr vorbeisehen.

In den westlichen Ländern organisierten sich Schüler, um gegen Prügelstrafe und Schuluniformen ihr Votum einzulegen. Hin und wieder las oder hörte man von 10jährigen, die ein Bankkonto eröffneten, von Eltern, die öffentlich angeklagt wurden, weil sie ihre Kinder mißhandelten oder auf sonst eine Weise unzulänglich behandelten. Die unschuldigen Kleinen waren im Begriff, ihre Erfahrungen in der großen Welt zu sammeln.

Doch all dies stand in keinem Verhältnis zu den erschütternden Nachrichten, die aus Afrika, Südamerika, China und aus dem Fernen Osten kamen. Die Erwachsenen mußten erkennen, daß in weiten Teilen der Erde Millionen von Kindern verhungerten, daß Sechsjährige in den Krieg zogen und daß es Kinderarbeit und Kinderprostitution gab.

Trotzdem gab es für die wenigen Glücklichen unter ihnen doch noch genügend Sonne und Zeit für ihre Kinderträume.

Les adultes aiment entourer l'enfance d'une aura de magie. Ils aiment se la remémorer comme une époque bénie où un bâton peut servir d'épée ou de trompette, un petit bois de château, un carton de Ferrari – une époque où le temps libre et le beau temps suffisaient pour pouvoir réaliser ses rêves.

Dans les années soixante-dix, ils eurent le plus grand mal à conserver cette image idyllique intacte. Dans un monde déjà saturé par l'omniprésente surveillance des caméras de télévision, les souffrances et les chagrins de l'enfance se retrouvèrent au premier plan.

A l'Ouest, les enfants s'organisèrent en syndicats et contestèrent certaines formes d'autorité, allant des sanctions disciplinaires aux uniformes. Des enfants de 10 ans ouvrirent des comptes en banque, des parents furent accusés ouvertement par leur progéniture de cruauté et d'incapacité. Les petits innocents qu'ils étaient, étaient en train d'acquérir l'expérience du monde.

Mais ce n'était rien comparé aux histoires accablantes provenant d'Afrique, d'Amérique du Sud, de Chine et d'Extrême-Orient. On s'aperçut que dans de nombreuses régions du monde, les enfants crevaient de faim par millions, que certains devenaient soldats à l'âge de six ans, que d'autres travaillaient et se prostituaient.

Néanmoins, pour ceux qui avaient la chance d'échapper à cette misère, il y avait encore assez de soleil et de temps.

Playing in the Troubles. Children in Belfast,
Northern Ireland use the wreckage of a
burnt-out van as their playground, 1975.
A year or two later and they may well have
been hurling stones at troops and police.

Spiele inmitten der Unruhen. Kinder in
der nordirischen Stadt Belfast benutzen das
ausgebrannte Wrack eines Autos als Spielplatz, 1975. Ein oder zwei Jahre später
werden sie vielleicht schon Steine gegen
Truppen und Polizisten geschleudert haben.

Jeux pendant les troubles. Des enfants de
Belfast, en Irlande du Nord, utilisent une
camionnette calcinée comme terrain de jeux,
1975. Dans un an ou deux, on les retrouvera
peut-être en train de lancer des pierres sur les
soldats et la police.

Watching the watchers... A pair of Belfast boys keep
a careful eye on soldiers of the Scots Greys
Regiment, 1970.

Die Beobachter beobachten ... Zwei kleine Jungen
aus Belfast werfen ein Auge auf die Soldaten des
Schottischen Grauen Regiments, 1970.

Veillant sur les veilleurs ... Deux gamins de Belfast
dévisagent attentivement des soldats du régiment des
Scots Greys, 1970.

A young warrior
takes to the streets
of Belfast armed
with a stick and a
dustbin lid, 1970.

Ein junger Krieger
zieht mit einem
Stock und einem
Mülleimerdeckel
bewaffnet durch die
Straßen von Belfast,
1970.

Un jeune guerrier
dans les rues de
Belfast, armé d'un
bâton et d'un
couvercle de
poubelle, 1970.

Children in the playground of a battered
wives' squat in Hartley Street, east London,
1978. The slogan on the wall in the
background tries to ensure that the space is
kept free.

Kinder auf dem Spielplatz eines Hauses für
mißhandelte Frauen in der Hartley Street im
Ostteil Londons, 1978. Die Aufschrift an der
Mauer weist darauf hin, daß dieser Platz für
Kinder bestimmt ist.

Des enfants sur le terrain d'un squat occupé
par des femmes battues, Hartley Street, est de
Londres, 1978. Le slogan apposé sur le mur
essaye de réserver cet espace aux enfants.

February 1974. The Noble Art of Kung Fu.
Michael Fresco's picture shows two girls in a
London park demonstrating their martial arts
skills. It's a far cry from Barbie Doll.

Februar 1974. Die hohe Kunst des Kung Fu.
Das Foto dieser beiden Mädchen, die in
einem Londoner Park ihre asiatischen
Kampfsportkünste demonstrieren, wurde von
Michael Fresco aufgenommen. Barbie Doll ist
weit weg.

Février 1974. Le noble art du Kung Fu. Cette
photographie de Michael Fresco montre deux
filles en pleine action dans un parc de
Londres. On est loin de la poupée Barbie!

Capitalist games. Eight-year-old Mark Harman from London enjoys a
game of Monopoly with his brother Graham and his sister Belinda,
May 1976. Mark spent six hours a week relaxing on his bed of nails.

Kapitalistische Spiele. Der achtjährige Mark Harman aus London
spielt mit seinem Bruder Graham und seiner Schwester Belinda
Monopoly, Mai 1976. Mark verbringt sechs Stunden pro Woche zur
Entspannung auf seinem Nagelkissen.

Jeux capitalistes. Mark Harman de Londres, huit ans, joue au
Monopoly avec son frère Graham et sa sœur Belinda, mai 1976. Mark
passait six heures par semaine à se relaxer sur un lit de clous.

Communist games. A teacher
uses a giant board to give his
pupils a chess lesson, Pskov,
USSR, April 1975.

Kommunistische Spiele. An
einer großen Schachtafel gibt
ein Lehrer seinen Schülern
eine Schachunterrichtsstunde,
Pskow, UdSSR, April 1975.

Jeux communistes. Un
professeur donne une leçon
d'échecs à ses élèves à Pskov,
URSS, avril 1975.

Young student…
A young Asian girl
at work during an
art class in a London
school, October
1972.

Junge Schülerin …
Ein kleines asiati-
sches Mädchen beim
Malunterricht in
einer Londoner
Schule, Oktober
1972.

Ecolière …
Une petite fille
asiatique lors d'une
leçon de peinture
dans une école
londonienne,
octobre 1972.

…Old Masters. A group of students make notes on some famous works of art during a visit to the National Gallery, London, March 1978. Art, music, dance and drama were educationally valued in the Seventies.

… Alte Meister. Eine Gruppe von Schülern macht sich Notizen zu einigen berühmten Werken während eines Besuches der National Gallery in London, März 1978. Kunst, Musik, Tanz und Theater waren in den siebziger Jahren wichtige Bestandteile des Unterrichts.

… Vieux maîtres. Un groupe d'écoliers prend des notes pendant une visite à la National Gallery de Londres, mars 1978. On accordait une place importante à l'art, la musique, la danse et au théâtre dans l'éducation des années soixante-dix.

Fiddlers three. Eamonn McCabe's study of
three budding musicians practising in their
garden, October 1979.

Die drei Fidler. Eamonn McCabe nahm das
Foto dieser drei Nachwuchsmusiker auf, die
im Garten fleißig üben, Oktober 1979.

Trois violonistes. Etude d'Eamonn McCabe
montrant trois musiciens en herbe dans leur
jardin, octobre 1979.

Six-year-old Melanie McLeod checks and tunes her steel pan before taking part in the Schools Steelband Festival at the Commonwealth Institute, London, 5 December 1979. Over 2,000 school children took part.

Die sechsjährige Melanie McLeod überprüft und stimmt ihr Stahlbecken bevor es beim Schools Steelband Festival im Londoner Commonwealth Institute losgeht, 5. Dezember 1979. An diesem Musikfest nahmen über 2.000 Schulkinder teil.

Melanie McLeod, six ans, accorde sa casserole en acier avant de participer au Steelband-Festival à l'Institut du Commonwealth, Londres, 5 décembre 1979. Plus de 2 000 élèves participèrent à cette manifestation.

British car, German
plates, Italian
clothes. A little boy
models clothes
for the House of
Jaeger, 1971.

Englisches Auto,
deutsche Ausstat-
tung, italienische
Kleidung. Ein
kleiner Junge führt
Kinderbekleidung
des Modehauses
Jaeger vor, 1971.

Voiture britannique,
plaques allemandes,
vêtements italiens.
Un petit garçon pose
pour la maison de
couture Jaeger,
1971.

Michele Durlow
bounces along on
her Spacehopper to
model clothes for
Littlewoods' Stores,
June 1971.

Michele Durlow
hopst auf einem
Hüpfball herum und
präsentiert dabei
Kinderkleidung aus
den Littlewoods'
Stores, Juni 1971.

Posant pour les
vêtements des ma-
gasins Littlewood,
Michele Durlow fait
des bonds sur son
ballon, juin 1971.

Ten-year-old Le Luy (right) and six-year-old Cu Van Anh (left) at an orphanage in Thi Nge, South Vietnam, February 1973. Both boys had lost their limbs in the Vietnam War.

Der zehnjährige Le Luy (rechts) und der sechsjährige Cu Van Anh (links) leben in einem Waisenhaus in Thi Nge in Südvietnam, Februar 1973. Beide Jungen haben ihre Gliedmaßen im Vietnamkrieg verloren.

Le Luy, dix ans (à droite) et Cu Van Anh, six ans (à gauche) à l'orphelinat de Thi Nge, Viêt-nam du Sud, février 1973. Les deux garçons ont perdu bras et jambe pendant la guerre du Viêt-nam.

One of the hundreds
of thousands of
young refugees from
Somalia, 1978.
The Ogaden war
ended in March of
that year, but the
suffering continued.

Eines von hundert-
tausenden von
somalischen
Flüchtlingskindern,
1978. Der Krieg von
Ogaden ging zwar
im März desselben
Jahres zu Ende,
doch das Leiden war
noch längst nicht
vorbei.

L'un des 100 000
réfugiés somaliens,
1978. La guerre
d'Ogaden se termina
en mars de la même
année, mais les
souffrances endurées
par la population
continuèrent.

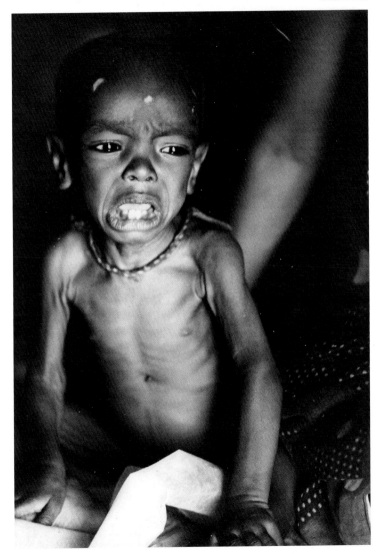

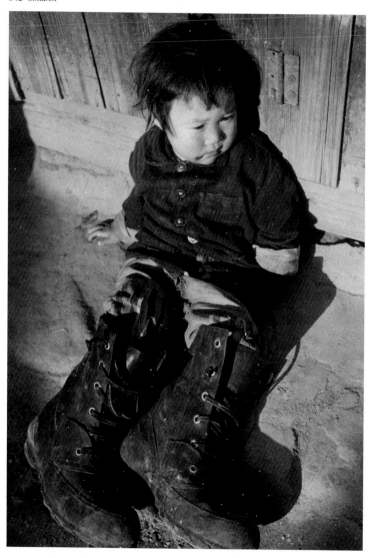

A tiny Korean boy tries vainly to fill his father's military boots, March 1970.

Ein kleiner Junge aus Korea probiert vergeblich die Militärstiefel seines Vaters an, März 1970.

Un tout petit bonhomme coréen essaye vainement de remplir les bottes militaires de son père, mars 1970.

1974. A group of orphans in Saigon, South Vietnam, waiting to have their hair washed, portrayed by Penny Tweedie. The war between North and South still had another bitter year to run.

1974. Penny Tweedie nahm diese Waisenkinder aus Saigon in Südvietnam auf, die auf ihre Haarwäsche warten. Der Krieg zwischen Nord- und Südvietnam sollte noch ein weiteres grausames Jahr andauern.

1974. Un groupe d'orphelins à Saigon, Viêt-nam du Sud, attendant qu'on leur lave les cheveux. Photographie de Penny Tweedie. La guerre entre le Nord et le Sud devait durer encore le temps d'une cruelle année.

A child soldier of the Marxist MPLA during the civil war in Angola, February 1976. This was real, not play.

Ein Kindersoldat der marxistischen MPLA im Bürgerkrieg von Angola, Februar 1976. Das ist kein Spiel, sondern bitterer Ernst.

Un enfant soldat du MPLA marxiste pendant la guerre civile en Angola, février 1976. Il ne s'agit pas d'un jeu, cette scène est bien réelle.

Chinese schoolchildren and members of the Communist Youth
Movement demonstrate their military skills in Hanking, April 1974.
The weapons are wooden dummies. They would not have had the
strength to lift genuine ones.

Chinesische Schulkinder und Mitglieder der kommunistischen Jugend-
bewegung demonstrieren in Hanking ihre militärischen Fähigkeiten,
April 1974. Die Waffen sind aus Holz, echte Waffen wären zu schwer
für sie gewesen.

Des écoliers chinois, membres du Mouvement de la jeunesse
communiste, font la démonstration de leur adresse militaire, Hanking,
avril 1974. Les armes en bois sont factices. Les écoliers n'auraient pas
eu la force de soulever des armes véritables.

A black and white friendship, South Africa, 1970. It embodied all that Apartheid fought so savagely to destroy.

Eine schwarz-weiße Freundschaft in Südafrika, 1970. Dieses Foto beinhaltet alles, was die Apartheid so grausam zu zerstören suchte.

Amitié blanche et noire, Afrique du Sud, 1970. Cette photographie incarne tout ce que l'apartheid s'efforçait sauvagement de détruire.

Wales, September 1979. Joy and innocence amidst the swings of a children's playground, Tiger Bay, Cardiff. The area around the docks of Tiger Bay was one of the most deprived areas of the Welsh capital.

Wales, September 1979. Unschuldige Fröhlichkeit bestimmt das Bild auf diesem Spielplatz bei Tiger Bay, Cardiff. Die Gegend um die Docks der Tiger Bay gehörte zu den heruntergekommensten Vierteln der walisischen Hauptstadt.

Pays de Galles, septembre 1979. Joie et innocence sur les balançoires d'un terrain de jeux, Tiger Bay, Cardiff. Ce quartier situé autour des docks de Tiger Bay était l'un des plus pauvres de la capitale galloise.

Lady Diana Spencer
(later Princess of
Wales), July 1970.
She was then nine
years old. The fame
and the pain lay
ahead.

Lady Diana Spencer
(spätere Prinzessin
von Wales), Juli
1970. Sie war da-
mals neun Jahre alt.
Berühmtheit und
Kummer lagen noch
vor ihr.

Lady Diana Spencer
(future princesse de
Galles), alors âgée
de neuf ans, juillet
1970. Un destin
tragique l'attend.

16-year-old William Hague receives a standing ovation at the Conservative Party Conference, Blackpool, England, 13 October 1977. The 'Churchillian boy wonder' later became leader of the Conservative Party.

Der 16jährige William Hague erhält auf dem Parteitag der Konservativen in Blackpool stehenden Beifall, England, 13. Oktober 1977. „Churchills Wunderknabe" wurde später Parteivorsitzender der Konservativen.

William Hague, 16 ans, très applaudi lors de la conférence du parti conservateur, Blackpool, Angleterre, 13 octobre 1977. « L'enfant prodige churchillien » devint plus tard le leader du parti conservateur.

12. All human life
Menschliches, Allzumenschliches
Les petits et les grands événements de la vie

Sweet dreams... Salome, a three-week-old baby gorilla, is put to bed in a carry cot, watched by a crowd of children at the Regent's Park Zoo, London, August 1976.

Schlaf gut ... Das drei Wochen alte Gorilla-Baby Salomé wurde in eine Kindertragetasche gebettet und von den umstehenden Kindern im Londoner Regent's Park Zoo bestaunt, August 1976.

Fais de beaux rêves ... Salomé, un bébé gorille de trois semaines, est couché dans un lit portable, veillé par une foule d'enfants au zoo de Regent's Park, Londres, août 1976.

12. All human life
Menschliches, Allzumenschliches
Les petits et les grands événements de la vie

The Seventies was the last decade in which many ancient assumptions could pass unchallenged. Never again could fur coats be paraded without fear of verbal, if not physical abuse for the wearer. Never again could naked models recline on the bonnets of gleaming limousines at motor shows without protest from militant feminists. Never again could hunters enjoy their pursuit without fear of saboteurs spoiling such sport.

People still did all sorts of silly things with animals, sausages and machines. People still invented strange gadgets that crept along the ground, or rose perilously in the air. The rich flaunted their wealth in ways that some envied, some despised, many mocked.

There were triumphs and disasters. Chay Blyth sailed alone around the world in 293 days. Mount Etna erupted. A cyclone ravaged the Northern Territory of Australia. Hurricane Gladys threatened the US coast but quietly died away over the Atlantic. Over 360 people were killed when a DC-10 crashed shortly after take-off from Orly Airport, Paris. 900 members of the People's Temple committed suicide by drinking cyanide in Jonestown, Guyana.

And Chi-Chi, the giant panda, died in London Zoo after 15 years in captivity – just as people began to challenge the whole concept of zoos.

Die siebziger Jahre waren die letzte Dekade, in der alte Gewohnheiten ohne Mißbilligung hingenommen wurden. Wer damals einen Pelzmantel trug, lief keine Gefahr, beschimpft oder gar tätlich angegriffen zu werden. Militante Feministinnen gingen noch nicht auf die Barrikaden, wenn sich nackte Models auf blitzblanken Kühlerhauben räkelten, und Jäger konnten ihrer Beschäftigung nachgehen ohne Angst vor Saboteuren ihres Sportes haben zu müssen.

Noch ließen sich die Menschen allerhand Unsinn einfallen, den sie mit Tieren, Würsten und Maschinen anstellen konnten. Sie erfanden seltsame technische Geräte, die auf der Erde entlang krochen oder sich auf gefährliche Art in die Lüfte erhoben. Die Reichen dieser Welt genossen ihren Wohlstand in einer Weise, um die sie manche beneideten, andere sie verachteten und wieder andere sich darüber lustig machen.

Man feierte Triumphe und beklagte Tragödien. Chay Blyth segelte in 293 Tagen um die Welt. Der Ätna spuckte Lava. Ein Wirbelsturm verwüstete das Nordterritorium Australiens. Der Hurrikan Gladys näherte sich bedrohlich der US-Küste, verlor sich dann aber doch über dem Atlantik. Über 360 Menschen starben bei dem DC-10-Unglück kurz nach dem Start vom Pariser Flughafen Orly. 900 Mitglieder der Sekte People's Temple begingen in Jonestown, Guyana, Selbstmord, indem sie Zyanid schluckten.

Und Chi-Chi, der Riesenpanda, starb nach 15jähriger Gefangenschaft im Zoo von London – gerade als man begann, das Konzept der Zoo-Tierhaltung in Frage zu stellen.

Les années soixante-dix furent la dernière décennie à voir incontestées d'anciennes habitudes. Plus jamais par la suite on ne pourrait porter de manteau de fourrure sans risquer de se faire insulter, sinon agresser. Plus jamais des mannequins nus ne pourraient s'étirer sur des capots de limousines au cours de salons automobiles sans encourir les protestations des féministes. Plus jamais les chasseurs ne pourraient pratiquer la chasse sans crainte d'être blâmés.

Des gens continuaient de faire de drôles de choses avec des animaux, des saucisses et des machines. D'autres continuaient d'inventer d'étranges gadgets qui rampaient sur le sol ou s'élevaient dangereusement dans les airs. Les riches faisaient étalage de leur richesse – enviée par certains, méprisée par d'autres, moquée par la plupart.

Il y eut des triomphes et des désastres. Chay Blyth accomplit en solitaire le tour du monde en bateau en 293 jours. L'Etna fit éruption. Un cyclone ravagea le territoire du nord de l'Australie. L'ouragan Gladys menaça la côte des Etats-Unis, mais s'essouffla au-dessus de l'Atlantique. Plus de 360 personnes furent tuées lors de l'accident du DC-10 peu après son décollage de l'aéroport d'Orly à Paris. 900 membres de la secte du Temple du peuple se suicidèrent au cyanure, à Jonestown en Guyane.

Et Chi-Chi, le panda géant, mourut dans le zoo de Londres après 15 ans de captivité – au moment même où on commençait à remettre en question le principe des zoos.

Christine Jorgensen, the first man to become a woman, holds a press reception at the London Pavilion cinema, September 1970.

Christine Jorgensen, der erste Mann, der zu einer Frau wurde, hier bei einem Presseempfang im Londoner Kino Pavillon, September 1970.

Christine Jorgensen, le premier homme à devenir une femme, organise une réception pour la presse au Pavillon du cinéma de Londres, septembre 1970.

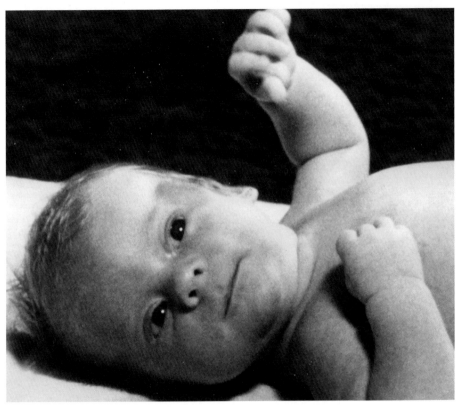

Louise Brown, the world's first test-tube baby, 3 September 1978. She was then five and a half weeks old. Louise was born in a Manchester hospital after 'in vitro' fertilization in a pioneering operation by Dr Patrick Steptoe.

Louise Brown war das erste Retorten-Baby, 3. September 1978. Sie war damals fünfeinhalb Wochen alt. Louise wurde nach einer „In-vitro"-Fertilisation durch Dr. Patrick Steptoe in einem Krankenhaus in Manchester geboren.

Louise Brown, le premier bébé-éprouvette, 3 septembre 1978. Elle était âgée de cinq semaines et demie. Louise naquit dans un hôpital de Manchester après une fécondation « in vitro » lors d'une opération avant-gardiste réalisée par le docteur Patrick Steptoe.

A police officer searches a Manchester United football fan, August 1974. This was part of an operation to prevent violence on the terraces.

Ein Polizist durch-sucht einen Fußball-fan von Manchester United, August 1974. Maßnahmen wie diese sollten gewalttätige Aus-schreitungen auf den Zuschauertribünen verhindern.

Un officier de police fouille un fan de l'équipe de football Manchester United, août 1974, dans le cadre d'une opéra-tion destinée à empêcher la violence dans les tribunes des stades.

Marion Broome waits to deposit gold bars at the Midland Bank, Earl's Court, London, February 1977. She had been modelling at the International Men's and Boys' Wear Exhibition – wearing very little but gold paint.

Marion Broome wartet am Schalter der Midland Bank um Goldbarren zu deponieren, Earl's Court, London, Februar 1977. Das Model der Internationalen Herrenbekleidungsausstellung hatte zwar nur wenig an, war dafür aber mit Gold bemalt.

Marion Broome dépose des lingots d'or au guichet de la Midland Bank, Earl's Court, Londres, février 1977. Elle était mannequin à l'Exposition internationale de la mode masculine – et ne portait quasiment que de la peinture d'or.

Hugh Hefner, President of Playboy Enterprises, relaxes with one of his 'playmates' in his luxury plane, Heathrow Airport, London, July 1970. Hefner's empire, founded on magazines, clubs and real estate, made him an extremely wealthy man.

Hugh Hefner, Präsident der Playboy Enterprises, entspannt sich zusammen mit einem seiner Playmates in seinem Luxus-Flieger, Flughafen Heathrow, London, Juli 1970. Seine Zeitschriften, Nachtclubs und Grundstücke hatten ihn zu einem überaus wohlhabenden Mann gemacht.

Hugh Hefner, président de Playboy Enterprises, se détend avec une de ses « playmates » dans son avion de luxe, aéroport de Heathrow, Londres, juillet 1970. L'empire de Hefner, basé sur des magazines, des clubs et de l'immobilier, faisait de lui un homme très riche.

Paris, June 1974. Millionaire ship-owner Aristotle Onassis 'parties'
with Italian film star Elsa Martinelli. Despite appearances to the
contrary, he was still mourning the death of his son in a plane crash
the previous year. Onassis died nine months later.

Paris, Juni 1974. Der millionenschwere Reeder Aristoteles Onassis in
Partystimmung mit dem italienischen Filmstar Elsa Martinelli. Auch
wenn es nicht so aussieht, trauert er immer noch um seinen Sohn, der
im Jahr zuvor bei einem Flugzeugunglück ums Leben gekommen war.
Neun Monate später starb Onassis.

Paris, juin 1974. L'armateur Aristotle Onassis en compagnie de la star
de cinéma italienne Elsa Martinelli lors d'une réception. En dépit des
apparences, il était encore en deuil de son fils tué dans un accident
d'avion l'année précédente. Onassis mourut neuf mois plus tard.

A symphony in tweed. Nobby Clark's picture of members of the Royal Family at the Badminton Horse Trials, Gloucestershire, April 1977. This was an annual event in the Royal Diary, though clearly not one that Princess Margaret (extreme right) looked forward to.

Symphonie in Tweed. Nobby Clark fotografierte die königliche Familie beim Springreiten von Badminton, Gloucestershire, April 1977. Die Veranstaltung stand alljährlich im Kalender der Royals, doch schien sich die Begeisterung von Prinzessin Margaret (ganz rechts) offensichtlich in Grenzen zu haltern.

Symphonie en tweed. Photographie de Nobby Clark montrant les membres de la famille royale lors du concours hippique de Badminton, Gloucestershire, avril 1977. Il s'agit d'un événement annuel dans le calendrier royal, mais la Princesse Margaret (tout à droite) cache bien son enthousiasme.

Anaheim, California, 1975. Emperor Hirohito of
Japan and Mickey Mouse meet at Disneyland.
Hirohito had long since denounced his legendary
divinity – unlike the Mouse.

Anaheim, Kalifornien, 1975. Der japanische
Kaiser Hirohito und Micky Maus begegnen sich
in Disneyland. Bescheidenheit gehörte zu den
Tugenden Hirohitos – ganz im Gegensatz
zur Maus.

Anaheim, Californie, 1975. L'empereur du Japon
Hirohito et Mickey Mouse se rencontrent à
Disneyland. Hirohito avait depuis longtemps
dénoncé sa propre divinité légendaire –
contrairement à Mickey.

London Underground, July 1974. Pop singer Desmond Decker (left) helps 'Mad' Eric Jarvis attempt to break the world record for Sewage Pipe Squatting.

Londoner U-Bahn, Juli 1974. Der Pop-sänger Desmond Decker (links) hilft „Mad" Eric Jarvis, den Weltrekord im Reinigen von ver-schmutzten Rohren zu brechen.

Dans le métro de Londres, juillet 1974. Le chanteur pop, Desmond Decker (à gauche) aide « Mad » Eric Jarvis à battre son record du monde d'occupation d'un tuyau d'égout.

May 1972. Doreen Maunsell, world champion haggis-eater, prepares to defend her title by consuming a 10lb haggis, Waterloo Station, London. A haggis is made from the heart, lungs and liver of a sheep or calf, mixed with oatmeal and onions.

Mai 1972. Doreen Maunsell, amtierende Weltmeisterin im Haggis-Essen, bereitet sich darauf vor, ihren Titel durch Vertilgen eines 10Pfünders zu verteidigen. Haggis werden aus Herz, Lunge und Leber von Schafen oder Kälbern gemacht, vermischt mit Hafermehl und Zwiebeln.

Mai 1972. Doreen Maunsell, championne du monde des mangeurs de haggis se prépare à défendre son titre en entamant un haggis de 10 livres, gare de Waterloo, Londres. Le haggis est un estomac de mouton rempli d'abats de mouton ou de veau, mélangés à de l'avoine et des oignons.

Mixed bathing.
Boris the Afghan
hound and
his owner share
the family bath,
May 1972.

Gemischtes Bad. Der
Afghanenrüde Boris
und sein Frauchen
teilen sich die Bade-
wanne, Mai 1972.

Bain mixte. Le
lévrier afghan Boris
et sa propriétaire
prennent leur bain
ensemble, mai 1972.

Five Highland
terriers arrive at
Cruft's Dog Show,
Kensington
Olympia, London,
5 February 1971.

Diese fünf
Highland-Terrier
kommen gerade von
der Hundeschau von
Cruft, Kensington
Olympia, London,
5. Februar 1971.

Des terriers de la
race Five Highland
arrivent pour parti-
ciper au salon du
chiens de Cruft,
Kensington
Olympia, Londres,
5 février 1971.

A novelty dog race. Frank Tewkesbury's picture of Afghan hounds bounding out of the traps at the Crayford Greyhound Stadium, September 1978. Afghans cannot match a greyhound's speed, and offer far more wind resistance speed.

Ein neuartiges Hunderennen. Dieses Foto von Frank Tewkesbury zeigt Afghanen beim Sprung aus der Box im Greyhound Stadium von Crayford, September 1978. Afghanen können mit der Schnelligkeit von Windhunden nicht mithalten, denn ihr Fell bietet einen viel größeren Windwiderstand.

Une nouvelle course de chiens. Photographie de Frank
Tewkesbury montrant des lévriers afghans bondissant de
leur trappe au stade de lévriers de Crayford, septembre
1978. Les lévriers afghans ne peuvent atteindre la vitesse des
lévriers, ils ont plus de résistance au vent.

Oxford Street, London, 1973. A line of
well-shod though immodest mannequins in
the window of the Bourne and
Hollingsworth department store.

Oxford Street, London, 1973. Die
Schaufensterpuppen des Kaufhauses Bourne
and Hollingsworth sind zwar gut beschuht,
aber ansonsten doch eher dürftig bekleidet.

Oxford Street, Londres, 1973. Une rangée
de mannequins bien chaussés mais
impudiques dans la vitrine du magasin
Bourne and Hollingsworth.

Claude Lalanne places another giant sardine in the tin for an exhibition of sculpture at the Whitechapel Art Gallery, east London, June 1976.

Claude Lalanne legt für eine Skulpturen-ausstellung in der Whitechapel Art Gallery eine weitere Riesensardine in die Konservenbüchse, London, Juni 1976.

Claude Lalanne met en place une autre sardine géante dans une boîte de conserve, dans le cadre de l'exposition de sculpture de la galerie Whitechapel Art, est de Londres, juin 1976.

Seesaw in the park. Mike Lloyd's picture of Rosie the
elephant tipping the balance as she settles on a park bench in
London, October 1977.

Wippe im Park. Als die Elefantendame Rosie auf diesem Foto
von Mike Lloyd sich auf einer Parkbank niederläßt, stört sie
die Balance doch empfindlich, London, Oktober 1977.

Jeu de bascule dans le parc. Photographie de Mike Lloyd
montrant Rosie l'éléphant faisant chavirer le banc d'un parc,
Londres, octobre 1977.

USA, January 1970. A young girl shares her box of popcorn with Billy the Kid at a zoo in Homosassa, Florida.

USA, Januar 1970. Ein kleines Mädchen teilt ihr Popcorn mit Billy the Kid in einem Zoo in Homosassa, Florida.

Etats-Unis, janvier 1970. Une petite fille partage son sac de popcorn avec Billy the Kid, zoo de Homosassa, Floride.

Plenty of room on top... An overcrowded
train arrives in Cairo, October 1970. The
passengers were mourners on their way to the
funeral of Gamal Abdel Nasser, President of
the United Arab Republic.

Auf dem Dach ist jede Menge Platz ... Dieser
völlig überfüllte Zug erreicht Kairo, Oktober
1970. Die Fahrgäste sind Trauernde auf
ihrem Weg zum Staatsbegräbnis Gamal Abdel
Nassers, Präsident der Vereinigten Arabischen
Republik.

De la place en haut ... Un train bondé arrive
au Caire, octobre 1970. Les passagers en deuil
se rendent aux funérailles de Gamal Abdel
Nasser, président de la République arabe unie.

...No room inside. A commuter makes a quick exit through the window of a train at a Tokyo station, April 1972. The train was unusually crowded due to a railway strike which had led to many cancellations.

... Kein Platz im Zug. Eine Pendlerin steigt auf einem Bahnhof in Tokio schnell aus dem Fenster aus, April 1972. Wegen eines Eisenbahnerstreiks waren viele Züge ausgefallen und viele Züge hoffnungslos überfüllt.

... Mais pas à l'intérieur. Une banlieusarde sort du train par une fenêtre, dans une station de Tokyo, avril 1972. Le train était bondé du fait d'une grève des chemins de fer.

I'm Freddie, fly me! Sir Frederick Alfred Laker spreads his
wings in front of Concorde at Heathrow Airport, London, 1978.
Laker founded his airline to offer passengers cut-price fares.

Ich bin Freddie, flieg' mit mir! Sir Frederick Alfred Laker breitet
seine Arme vor einer Concorde auf dem Londoner Flughafen
Heathrow aus, 1978. Laker gründete eine eigene Fluggesellschaft,
mit der er verbilligte Flugpreise anbot.

Je suis Freddie, volez avec moi ! Sir Frederick Alfred Laker déploie
ses ailes devant le Concorde à l'aéroport de Heathrow, Londres,
1978. Laker fonda sa ligne aérienne pour offrir des tarifs bon
marché aux passagers.

June 1978. Holidaymakers sleep away the hours of tedium in the passenger lounge at Heathrow. They are waiting for flights that had been delayed by the industrial action of French air traffic controllers.

Juni 1978. Urlauber dösen aus Langeweile in der Wartehalle des Flughafens Heathrow vor sich hin. Sie warten auf ihre Flüge, die sich aufgrund eines Streiks der französischen Fluglotsen verspätet haben.

Juin 1978. Des vacanciers dorment dans la salle d'attente de Heathrow. Ils attendent leur vol retardé du fait d'une grève des contrôleurs aériens français.

December 1970. A heavy-duty Sikorsky S-64 Skycrane delivers from
factory to site a house measuring 44 feet by 28 feet. The process was part
of a scheme to provide instant housing in the United States.

Dezember 1970. Der Hochleistungshubschrauber Sikorsky S-64 Skycrane
liefert ein Haus von der Größe von 13 x 8,5 Meter direkt ab Fabrik.
Dieses Verfahren war Teil eines Projekts für Fertighäuser in den USA.

Décembre 1970. Un hélicoptère Sikorsky S-64 Skycrane livre depuis
l'usine une maison mesurant 13 mètres sur 8,5 mètres. Il s'agissait de
promouvoir les maisons instantanées aux Etats-Unis.

Marriage lines…
Tsen Hai Sun and
Hay Gy Sun
exchange wedding
rings as they hang
by their hair during
the ceremony
at Hassloch, Pfalz,
West Germany,
1979.

Hochzeitsbanden …
Tsen Hai Sun und
Hay Gy Sun
tauschen bei ihrer
Hochzeit ihre Ehe-
ringe während sie
an ihren Haaren
hängen, Hassloch,
Pfalz, Deutschland,
1979.

Liens du mariage …
Tsen Hai Sun et Hay
Gy Sun échangent
leurs alliances alors
qu'ils sont suspendus
par les cheveux
pendant la cérémo-
nie de leur mariage,
Hassloch, Pfalz,
Allemagne de
l'Ouest, 1979.

Challenging gravity… A burly contestant flexes his muscles in the traditional (and seemingly pointless) Swiss sport of 'Throwing the Stone', August 1977.

Die Schwerkraft herausfordern … Ein Teilnehmer läßt seine Muskeln in der traditionellen (und wohl bedeutungslosen) Schweizer Sportart „Steinwurf" spielen, August 1977.

Défiant la gravité … Un gaillard de forte carrure gonfle ses muscles pendant une démonstration du sport traditionnel suisse (et plutôt inutile), le « lancer de pierre », août 1977.

...and surviving. Eddie Kidd, English motorcyclist, successfully leaps the 80 feet span of a broken railway bridge, Maldon, Essex, December 1979. It was part of a stunt for the science-fiction film *Heavy Metal*.

... und überleben. Der englische Motorradfahrer Eddie Kidd schafft den Sprung über eine 24 Meter breite Kluft einer ehemaligen Eisenbahnbrücke, Maldon, Essex, Dezember 1979. Dies war einer der Stunts in dem Science-fiction-Streifen *Heavy Metal*.

... et survivant. Eddie Kidd, motocycliste anglais, bondit, avec succès, d'un pilier à l'autre, Maldon, Essex, décembre 1979. Entre ces deux piliers d'un pont ferroviaire détruit, il y avait plus de 24 mètres de vide. Il s'agissait d'une acrobatie réalisée pour le film de science-fiction *Heavy Metal*.

Testing the company's wares... A workman
takes time off to relax outside a factory in
Islington, London, 1970.

Die Produkte seiner Firma ausprobieren ...
Ein Arbeiter legt außerhalb der Fabrik eine
Pause ein, Islington, London, 1970.

Contrôle des marchandises ... Un ouvrier
s'accorde une petite sieste devant la porte de
son usine, Islington, Londres, 1970.

Testing the company's springs... American wrestlers the McGuire brothers set out to tour Japan by motorbike, March 1974. The brothers weighed 47 stone (300 kilos) and 41 stone (259 kilos) respectively.

Die Stoßfedern der Firma ausprobieren ... Die Brüder McGuire, amerikanische Ringkämpfer, begeben sich mit dem Motorrad auf Japan-Tour, März 1974. Die Brüder wogen 300 beziehungsweise 259 Kilogramm.

Test des produits ... Des lutteurs américains, les frères McGuire, entament leur tournée du Japon en moto, mars 1974. Les frères pesaient respectivement 300 et 259 kilos.

A bad year for snow? Members of the French long-distance ski team practice on the running track at the French National Institute of Sport, October 1971. They were preparing for the Winter Olympics in Japan.

Ein schlechtes Jahr für Schnee? Mannschaftsmitglieder der französischen Skilangläufer trainieren auf der Rennstrecke der nationalen französischen Sporthochschule, Oktober 1971. Sie bereiteten sich auf die Winterolympiade in Japan vor.

Pas de neige cette année ? Des membres de l'équipe française de ski de fond s'entraînent sur la piste de l'Institut national de sport français, octobre 1971. Ils préparent les Jeux olympiques d'hiver du Japon.

December 1978. The Grandville Wizards drive their 'skatecars' round the track at Brand's Hatch, Kent. Skatecars developed from skateboards. They were less than 20 inches high and 100 inches long, but had a top speed of 60mph.

Dezember 1978. Die Grandville Wizards umrunden mit ihren „Skatecars" die Rennstrecke von Brand's Hatch, Kent. Skatecars wurden aus Skateboards entwickelt. Sie waren knapp 50 Zentimeter hoch und 2,5 Meter lang, erreichten jedoch eine Spitzengeschwindigkeit von fast 100 km/h.

Décembre 1978. Les Wizards de Grandville conduisent leur « skatecar » sur la piste de Brand's Hatch, Kent. Les skatecars étaient une adaption des skateboards. Ces engins mesuraient moins de 50 cm de haut et 2,5 mètres de long, mais pouvaient atteindre une vitesse de 100 km/heure.

London, September 1977. The first combined computer, calculator and wristwatch goes on show at the International Watch and Jewellery Trades Fair, Wembley. It was known as 'Pulsar'.

London, September 1977. Die erste Armbanduhr mit Taschen-rechner wird auf der Internationalen Uhren- und Schmuckmesse in Wembley vorgestellt. Sie wurde unter der Bezeichnung „Pulsar" bekannt.

Londres, septembre 1977. La première montre-bracelet combinant un ordinateur et une calculatrice à la foire internationale des montres et bijoux de Wembley. Elle s' appelait « Pulsar ».

USA, January 1972. An engineer displays an early
integrated circuit at the molecular electronics division
of Westinghouse Electric, Elkridge, Maryland.

USA, Januar 1972. Ein Ingenieur der Molekular-
elektronik-Abteilung der Firma Westinghouse Electric
mit Sitz in Elkridge, Maryland, stellt einen der ersten
integrierten Schaltkreise vor.

Etats-Unis, janvier 1972. Un ingénieur met en place
l'un des premiers circuits intégrés dans le départe-
ment d'électronique moléculaire de l'usine
Westinghouse Electric, Elkridge, Maryland.

Beauty and the Beast… Helen Jones and Sue Shaw raise
the tone of the Motor Show at Earl's Court, London,
October 1971. Stunts such as this finally disproved the
notion that cars could be seen as phallic symbols.

Die Schöne und das Biest … Helen Jones und Sue Shaw
heben das Niveau dieser Autoaustellung von Earl's
Court, London, Oktober 1971. Nummern wie diese
widerlegten schließlich die Vorstellung, das Auto sein ein
Phallussymbol.

La Belle et la Bête … Helen Jones et Sue Shaw font
monter le ton du salon automobile de Earl's Court,
Londres, octobre 1971. De telles actions réfutaient
finalement la notion de symbole phallique des voitures.

…Beasts and the Beast. A family of baboons out for a day's motoring at the Windsor safari park, near London, October 1970. There seems to be some confusion as to who has the keys.

… Die Biester und das Biest. Diese Pavianfamilie macht eine Spritztour durch den Windsor-Safaripark nahe London, Oktober 1970. Die Frage ist nur, wer den Schlüssel hat.

… Les Bêtes et la Bête. Une famille de babouins en balade en voiture dans le parc safari de Windsor, près de Londres, octobre 1970. Mais qui a donc les clés ?

A new recruit being baptized by Jehovah's Witnesses in a
special tank at the Rugby Football ground, Twickenham,
London, August 1974. Frank Tewkesbury took the picture.

Ein Neuaufgenommener wird von den Zeugen Jehovas in
einem Spezialbecken auf dem Rubgy-Fußballfeld getauft,
Twickenham, London, August 1974. Das Foto nahm Frank
Tewkesbury auf.

Une nouvelle recrue est baptisée par des Témoins de
Jéhovah dans une cuve installée sur le terrain de football et
de rugby de Twickenham, Londres, août 1974. Photographie de Frank Tewkesbury.

A crowd gathers to watch a car sinking into a large puddle caused by subsidence in Zurich, Switzerland, August 1974. The crater opened when a water main burst.

Eine Gruppe Schaulustiger beobachtet, wie in Zürich ein Auto in der riesigen Wasserlache versinkt, die durch eine Erdabsenkung entstanden war, Schweiz, August 1974. Der Krater öffnete sich, nachdem ein Hauptwasserrohr gebrochen war.

Une foule contemple une voiture qui s'enfonce dans une grosse mare d'eau due à un affaissement de terrain provoqué par la rupture d'une canalisation principale, Zurich, Suisse, août 1974.

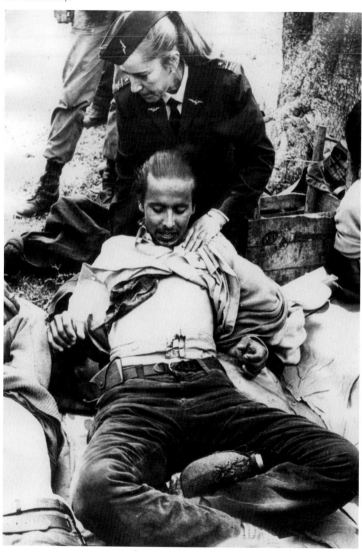

One of the survivors
of a plane crash
is brought down
from the Andes
Mountains,
Uruguay, March
1973.

Abtransport von
einem der Über-
lebenden eines Flug-
zeugunglücks in den
Anden, Uruguay,
März 1973.

L'un des survivants
d'un accident
d'avion dans les
Andes est transporté
en lieu sûr, Uruguay,
mars 1973.

The wreckage of the plane in the Andes. The survivors had waited 70 days to be rescued, and had been reduced to eating parts of the dead passengers. Both pictures were taken by Goksin Sipahioglu.

Das Wrack des in den Anden abgestürzten Flugzeugs. Die Überlebenden hatten 70 Tage auf ihre Bergung gewartet. Um nicht zu verhungern, mußten sie Teile ihrer toten Mitpassagiere essen. Beide Fotos stammen von Goksin Sipahioglu.

Epave de l'avion dans les Andes. Les survivants attendirent 70 jours avant d'être secourus et en furent réduits à manger les passagers morts. Les deux photographies furent prises par Goksin Sipahioglu.

10 Polish seamen were drowned when their trawler collapsed in gale
force winds in the Outer Hansthelm harbour, Denmark, 1974.
Another 17 members of the crew were rescued by helicopter.

10 polnische Seeleute ertranken, als ihr Schlepper vom Sturm ergriffen
wurde und im Außenhafen von Hansthelm kenterte, Dänemark, 1974.
Die anderen 17 Besatzungsmitglieder konnten mit Hubschraubern
gerettet werden.

10 marins polonais furent noyés lors du naufrage de leur chalutier,
pendant une forte tempête, dans le port d'Outer Hansthelm,
Danemark, 1974. Les 17 autres marins furent évacués par hélicoptère.

Army fire fighters battle with the scorching inferno that followed a natural gas explosion in southern Hungary, 1979.

Feuerwehrleute der Armee kämpfen gegen das Flammen-inferno an, das durch eine natür-liche Gasexplosion im Süden Ungarns entstanden war, 1979.

Des pompiers de l'armée combattent l'enfer torride provoqué par une explosion de gaz naturel dans le sud de la Hongrie, 1979.

Index

Abba 223
Abzug, Bella 130
Ali, Muhammad 305-7
Allen, Woody 170
Allende, Salvador 34-5, 100-1
Amin, Idi 28
Annis, Francesca 172
Arafat, Yasser 24
Austin, Tracy 293

Baader, Andreas 110
Bacon, Francis 199
Bailey, David 198
Bardot, Brigitte 186
Baryshnikov, Mikhail 210
Beaufort, Duke of 360
Begin, Menachem 25
Berger, Warren 18
Bernstein, Leonard 208-9
Bhutto, Zulfikar Ali 38
Biko, Steve 32
Bokassa, Jean-Bédel 29
Bolan, Marc 213
Botha, Piet 33
Boulez, Pierre 207
Bowie, David 217
Brandt, Willy 45
Brezhnev, Leonid 20-1
Brown, Louise 355
Bugner, Joe 309

Can 237
Carlos the Jackal 109
Carter, Jimmy 25
Castro, Fidel 34-5
Chappell, Greg 316
Chirac, Jaques 36
Christo, Javacheff 200-1
Collins, Phil 234
Comaneci, Nadia 303
Connors, Jimmy 297

Coppola, Francis Ford 161
Costello, Elvis 239
Cruyff, Johan 299
Curry, John 321
Curry, Tim 177
Czukay, Holger 237

Daly, Father Edward 65
Decker, Desmond 362
Deng Xiaoping 46
De Niro, Robert 161, 184
Devlin, Bernadette 134
Dury, Ian 236

Eastwood, Clint 166
Eisenhower, David 19
Elizabeth II, Queen 42, 360
Elizabeth, Queen Mother 360
Evert, Chris 296-7

Fonda, Jane 189
Ford, Betty 18
Ford, Gerald 18, 20-1
Frazier, Joe 304

Gaddafi, Colonel Muammar 22
Gowon, General Yakubu 31

Hackman, Gene 183
Hague, William 349
Harry, Debbie 238
Hearst, Patty 108
Heath, Edward 41
Hefner, Hugh 172, 358
Hirohito, Emperor 361
Hockney, David 191
Hoffman, Dustin 175

Jackson Five, The 225
Jackson, Michael 225
Jackson, Randy 229

Jagger, Mick 216
Jarvis, Eric 362
John, Elton 222
John Paul II 44
Jones, Allen 196
Jones, Tom 220
Jorgensen, Christine 354

Keaton, Diane 171
Keegan, Kevin 287
Khaled, Leila 103
Khomeini, Ayatollah 13, 26-7
Kidd, Eddie 379
Kilburn and the High Roads 236
Kinski, Nastassja 188
Kissinger, Henry 23
Kohl, Helmut 37
Korbut, Olga 302
Kubrick, Stanley 169
Kundera, Milan 203

Laker, Sir Freddie 374
Leone, Sergio 167
Lin Qui, Madame 129

McEnroe, John 295
MacGowan, Shane 240
McGuire Brothers 381
MacLaine, Shirley 180
MacLaren, Malcolm 263
Macmillan, Harold 41
Maier, Sepp 301
Mailer, Norman 205
Margaret, Princess 360
Marley, Bob 228
Martinelli, Elsa 359
Meinhof, Ulrike 111
Meir, Golda 47
Merckx, Eddie 308
Milovskaya, Galina 246
Minnelli, Liza 179
Mobutu Sese Seke 30, 307
Moro, Aldo 113-15

Nastase, Ilie 294
Navratilova, Martina 292
Newton-John, Olivia 178, 221
Nicholson, Jack 168
Nijinsky 312
Nixon, Richard 16-17, 19
Nureyev, Rudolf 211

Oldenburg, Claes 202
Oldfield, Mike 235
Onassis, Aristotle 359
O'Neal, Ryan 181
Osmonds, The 224
Owens, James 311

Pacino, Al 182
Pelé 300
Piggott, Lester 312
Polanski, Roman 172, 188
Pol Pot 60-1
Presley, Elvis 218

Redford, Robert 174
Redgrave, Vanessa 129
Red Rum 313
Reynolds, Burt 179
Richard, Cliff 221
Rifal, Abdul Monein 24
Riley, Bridget 194-5
Rosselini, Isabella 173
Rotten, Johnny 241

Schmidt, Helmut 39-40
Schleyer, Hanns-Martin 112
Scorsese, Martin 173
Schwarzenegger, Arnold 176
Sex Pistols, The 241
Siddigui, General Abdul 83
Sly and the Family Stone 230

Solzhenitsyn, Alexander
   204
Spencer, Lady Diana 348
Spitz, Mark 290-1
Stallone, Sylvester 185
Stern, Isaac 206
Stewart, Rod 219
Streep, Meryl 187
Streisand, Barbara 181
Sutch, Screaming Lord
131
Sutherland, Donald 180

Thatcher, Margaret 40,
43, 349
Three Degrees, The 232
Travolta, John 178
Truffaut, François 165
Turner, Tina 233

Viren, Lasse 310

Warhol, Andy 197
Welles, Orson 164
Westwood, Vivienne 262
White, Barry 231
Windsor, Wallis Duchess of
   42
Wyngarde, Peter 254

gettyimages

Over 70 million images and 30,000 hours of film footage are held by the various collections owned by Getty Images. These cover a vast number of subjects from the earliest photojournalism to current press photography, sports, social history and geography. Getty Images' conceptual imagery is renowned amongst creative end users.
www.gettyimages.com

Über 70 Millionen Bilder und 30 000 Stunden Film befinden sich in den verschiedenen Archiven von Getty Images. Sie decken ein breites Spektrum an Themen ab – von den ersten Tagen des Fotojournalismus bis hin zu aktueller Pressefotografie, Sport, Sozialgeschichte und Geographie. Bei kreativen Anwendern ist das Material von Getty Images für seine ausdrucksstarke Bildsprache bekannt.
www.gettyimages.com

Plus de 70 millions d'images et 30 000 heures de films sont détenus par les différentes collections dont Getty Images est le propriétaire. Cela couvre un nombre considérable de sujets – des débuts du photojournalisme aux photographies actuelles de presse, de sport, d'histoire sociale et de géographie. Le concept photographique de Getty Images est reconnu des créatifs.
www.gettyimages.com

Page/reference number

Description

CSV Marine rescues woman
     (Cover)
2SV Topless hippie
     (Frontispiece)

Chapter 1

13SV Ayatollah Khomeini
16SV Richard Nixon, Ohio
18SV Ford swearing in
19SV Nixon resigns
20SV Ford and Brezhnev
22SV Colonel Gaddafi
23SV Henry Kissinger
24SV Arafat and Rifal
25SV Carter and Begin
26SV Khomeini in garden, Paris
28SV Idi Amin Dada
29SV Jean-Bédel Bokassa

30SV Mobutu Sese Seko
31SV General Yakubu Gowon
32SV Body of Steve Biko
33SV Piet Botha
34SV Castro and Allende
36SV Jacques Chirac
37SV Helmut Kohl
38SV Zulfikar Ali Bhutto
39SV Helmut Schmidt
40SV Schmidt and Thatcher
41SV Macmillan and Heath
42SV Elizabeth II and Wallis
43SV Margaret Thatcher
44SV Pope John Paul II
45SV Willy Brandt
46SV Deng Xiaoping
47SV Golda Meir

Chapter 2

49SV Badly wounded soldier
52SV Blindfolded prisoners
53SV Marine rescues woman
54SV North Vietnamese troops, Laos

55SV Two Vietcong troops
56SV Vietcong greet prisoners
58SV Khmer Rouge soldier
59SV Injured children, Cambodia
60SV Pol Pot patrol
62SV Mass grave, Cambodia
63SV Khmer Rouge woman and baby
64SV Taking cover
65SV Father Edward Daly
66SV Belfast teenager arrested
67SV Injured man arrested, Belfast
68SV Troops occupy housing estate
70SV Petrol bombers
71SV Stone throwers
72SV Woman watching soldiers
73SV IRA bomb victim
74SV Iranian women
76SV Helicopter, Afghanistan
77SV Unexploded Iraqi bomb
78SV Egyptian prisoners
79SV Soldier watches Skyhawk plane
80SV Victim, Cyprus
81SV Running for cover, Nicosia

82SV   Bengali collaborators
83SV   Executing Bengali collaborators
84SV   Gun battle, Beirut
86SV   Woman pleading, Beirut
87SV   Bomb ruins, Beirut
88SV   UNITA guerrillas
89SV   Child soldiers, Southern Sudan
90SV   Look of suffering, Angola
91SV   Execution, Uganda
92SV   Soweto riots
93SV   Soweto riots, aerial view
94SV   Satirical demo, El Salvador
96SV   Mother with picture, El Salvador
97SV   Corpses, San Salvador
98SV   Sandinista rebel, Nicaragua
99SV   Gaol, Nicaragua
100SV   Salvador Allende

Chapter 3

103SV   Leila Khaled
106SV   Burning planes, North Jordan
108SV   Patty Hearst
109SV   Carlos the Jackal
110SV   Andreas Baader
111SV   Ulrike Meinhof
112SV   Hanns-Martin Schleyer
113SV   Aldo Moro
114SV   Body of Aldo Moro
116SV   Blindfolded hostage
117SV   Black September terrorist
118SV   Birmingham pub ruins
119SV   Bomb survivor, Guildford
120SV   Body of terrorist
121SV   Gun battle, Iraqi Embassy, Paris

Chapter 4

123SV   British Movement member
*   Kent State shootings
128SV   Vietnam veterans, Washington
129SV   Vanessa Redgrave leading demo
130SV   Bella Abzug
131SV   'Screaming Lord Sutch'
132SV   Gay rights march, New York
133SV   Gay Liberation Front, London
134SV   Bernadette Devlin
135SV   Cell walls, Maze Prison
136SV   Notting Hill Carnival riots
138SV   'I am British'
139SV   Tattooed skinhead
140SV   Enoch Powell supporters
141SV   Black People's Alliance march
142SV   Photographing an arrest
144SV   Burning sign
145SV   Jeering students
146SV   'Ian Smith – wanted for murder'
147SV   White Rhodesians
148SV   Protester arrested, Grunwick

149SV   Picket, Surrey Docks
150SV   Japanese commuters
151SV   'Bullet Trains'
152SV   Nurse and baby
153SV   Workers keeping warm
154SV   Piles of rubbish
156SV   Babies on placards
157SV   Waste paper demonstration
158SV   Seal
159SV   *Amoco Cadiz*

Chapter 5

161SV   Ford Coppola and de Niro
164SV   Orson Welles
165SV   François Truffaut
166SV   Clint Eastwood
167SV   Sergio Leone
168SV   Jack Nicholson
169SV   Stanley Kubrick
170SV   Woody Allen
171SV   Diane Keaton
172SV   Polanski, Hefner and Annis
173SV   Rossellini and Scorsese
174SV   Robert Redford
175SV   Dustin Hoffman
176SV   Arnold Schwarzenegger
177SV   Tim Curry
178SV   Newton-John and Travolta
179SV   Reynolds and Minnelli
180SV   Sutherland and MacLaine
181SV   O'Neal and Streisand
182SV   Al Pacino
183SV   Gene Hackman
184SV   Robert de Niro
185SV   Sylvester Stallone
186SV   Brigitte Bardot
187SV   Meryl Streep
188SV   Polanski and Kinski
189SV   Jane Fonda

Chapter 6

191SV   David Hockney
194SV   Bridget Riley
196SV   Allen Jones
197SV   Andy Warhol
198SV   David Bailey
199SV   Francis Bacon
200SV   Christo Javacheff
202SV   Claes Oldenburg
203SV   Milan Kundera
204SV   Alexander Solzhenitsyn
205SV   Norman Mailer
206SV   Erich Auerbach
207SV   Pierre Boulez
208SV   Leonard Bernstein
210SV   Mikhail Baryshnikov
211SV   Rudolf Nureyev

Chapter 7

213SV   Marc Bolan
216SV   Mick Jagger
217SV   David Bowie
218SV   Elvis Presley
219SV   Rod Stewart
220SV   Tom Jones
221SV   Richard and Newton-John
222SV   Elton John
223SV   Abba
224SV   The Osmonds
225SV   The Jackson Five
226SV   David Cassidy fans
227SV   Bay City Rollers fans
228SV   Bob Marley
229SV   Randy Jackson
230SV   Sly and the Family Stone
231SV   Barry White
232SV   The Three Degrees
233SV   Tina Turner
234SV   Phil Collins
235SV   Mike Oldfield
236SV   Ian Dury
237SV   Can
238SV   Debbie Harry
239SV   Elvis Costello
240SV   Shane MacGowan
241SV   The Sex Pistols

Chapter 8

243SV   Corduroy jackets
246SV   Fur and rocket
247SV   Satin trousers
248SV   Mini and platforms
249SV   Hippie with skullcap
250SV   John Bates knitwear
251SV   Mary Quant spring wear
252SV   Yamamoto knitwear
253SV   'Lick me all over 20$'
254SV   Peter Wyngarde
255SV   'Hot pants'
256SV   Striped socks
257SV   Denim vest and trouser
258SV   Couple, St Tropez
259SV   Gingham platforms
260SV   Fur coats
261SV   Astrakhan cape
262SV   Vivienne Westwood
263SV   Malcolm MacLaren

Chapter 9

265SV   Punk, Stockholm
268SV   Hippies, Bardney Pop Festival
270SV   Kissing, Isle of Wight
271SV   Vespa scooter
272SV   Hippie wedding
274SV   Honda chopper

275SV Fighting, Weeley Pop Festival
276SV Squatters
277SV King-size joint
278SV Pop fans at Windsor Great Park
280SV Skinheads outside a pub
281SV Holland Park pupils
282SV Fans rip up seating
283SV Angry skinhead
284SV 'No future'
285SV 'Bollocks to you all'

Chapter 10
287SV Kevin Keegan
290SV Mark Spitz
292SV Martina Navratilova
293SV Tracy Austin
294SV Ilie Nastase
295SV John McEnroe
296SV Chris Evert
297SV Connors and Evert
298SV Lazio playing Inter Milan
299SV Johan Cruyff
300SV Pelé
301SV Sepp Maier
302SV Olga Korbut
303SV Nadia Comaneci
304SV Joe Frazier
305SV Muhammad Ali
306SV Ali playfighting with child
307SV Ali and Mobutu
308SV Eddie Merckx
309SV Joe Bugner
310SV Lasse Viren
311SV James Owens
312SV Nijinsky
313SV Red Rum
314SV West Indian cricket supporters
315SV Scottish football fans
316SV Streaker, Brisbane
317SV Streaker, London
318SV Streaker, Montreal Olympics
320SV Ski acrobat
321SV John Curry

Chapter 11
323SV Child models
326SV Burnt-out van, Belfast
328SV Boys with soldiers, Belfast
329SV Armed with dustbin lid
330SV 'This is a playground not a
        carpark'
331SV Kung Fu
332SV Bed of nails
333SV Chess lesson
334SV Art class
335SV National Gallery
336SV Child violinists

337SV Steel pan
338SV Jaeger model
339SV Spacehopper
340SV Missing limbs
341SV Somalian refugee
342SV Father's boots
343SV Saigon orphans
344SV Child MPLA soldier
345SV Communist Youth Movement
346SV Black and white friendship
347SV Swings, Wales
348SV Lady Diana Spencer
349SV William Hague

Chapter 12
351SV Baby Gorilla
354SV Christine Jorgensen
355SV Louise Brown
356SV Police search
357SV Gold painted woman
358SV Hugh Hefner
359SV Aristotle Onassis
360SV The Royals kneeling
361SV Hirohito and Mickey Mouse
362SV Sewage pipe squatting
363SV Haggis-eater
364SV Dog bath
365SV Highland terriers
366SV Afghan hound race
368SV Mannequins
369SV Giant sardines
370SV Elephant
371SV Pop corn
372SV Overcrowded train, Cairo
373SV Overcrowded train, Tokyo
374SV Sir Freddie Laker
375SV Sleeping at Heathrow
376SV Sikorsky S-64 Skycrane
377SV Suspended by hair
378SV 'Throwing the Stone'
379SV Eddie Kidd
380SV Workman sleeping
381SV McGuire brothers
382SV Ski practice
383SV 'Skatecars'
384SV Digital watch
385SV Integrated circuit
386SV Naked girls on a car
387SV Baboons on car
388SV Baptism
389SV Sinking car
390SV Survivor, Andes Mountains
391SV Wreckage, Andes Mountains
392SV Collapsed trawler
393SV Gas explosion

Acknowledgements

Alan Band 166, 181, 376, 385
Consolidated News Pictures 18-21,
    108, 128
Gamma Liaison 16-17, 34-5, 58-61,
    76, 84-5, 87, 94-9, 120-1, 130,
    161, 171, 175, 179, 183-4,
    186-7, 200-3, 211, 303, 310-11,
    390-1
Peter Gould 178, 189, 218
The Observer 29, 38, 41, 43, 56-7,
    63, 72, 81-2, 133, 138, 142-5,
    147, 156-8, 207, 271, 277, 287,
    299, 304-5, 312, 321, 336, 341,
    343, 347, 360, 372

Pictures from other sources

Topham Picturepoint 126-7